Ecological Consequences of Climate Change

2012

Also by J. Emil Morhardt

Ecological Consequences of Climate Change

2012

A Roberts Environmental Center Annual Snapshot

J. Emil Morhardt, Editor

The Roberts Environmental Center Press

Roberts Environmental Center Press
Claremont McKenna College
925 N. Mills Avenue
Claremont, California 91711
(909) 621-8190

Morhardt, J. Emil
Ecological Consequences of Climate Change
2012: A Roberts Environmental Center Annual Snapshot/ J. Emil
Morhardt, Editor.

ISBN 978-0-9843823-5-4   (paper)

Table of Contents

Forward

J. Emil Morhardt

This is the ninth of the books published by the Roberts Environmental Center on various aspects of global climate change, analyzing and summarizing a selection of the papers published in scientific technical journals over the previous year. It deals with a small subset of the biological and ecological topics that could be covered, but deals with them in enough depth that the reader should come away with a clear view of the magnitude of the potential problems associated with anthropogenic (man-made) global warming from burning fossil fuels and the subsequent climate change. I write this contemporaneously with the 2011 United Nation climate talks being held in Durban, South Africa. The mood in the climate community is not particularly good; climate change has largely been eclipsed by global economic uncertainty in the public mind—enough so that you hardly hear anything about it from the Republican candidates who have been debating seemingly weekly all fall, and many of whom in previous years would have been strongly denouncing the very idea of anthropogenic climate change. But to the extent that it is in the public mind, the recent release of the second round of stolen emails from climate scientists at the University of East Anglia doesn't help their credibility, or the credibility of climate change itself, with the public and the skeptics.

Nevertheless, studies of the biological and ecological effects of increasing levels of greenhouse gas, global warming, and climate change are proceeding apace. The 50-some papers that are reviewed here address a wide range of concerns, some of which seem not so threatening in the short term (such as that increasing CO_2 concentrations are offsetting the adverse effects of temperature in many plant species for the moment) and others somewhat frightening (the increasing size of wildfires globally, for example). In the middle are disturbing topics such as the shifting of ecological range of many species and a general decrease in biodiversity in many places, accompanied by inevitable extinctions, both in the terrestrial and marine environments, and the uncertain effects of climate change on human migration,

This book is intended for non-scientists interested in getting a little more technical information than is possible in the popular media, but less than from trying to read papers in *Science*, *Nature*, or *Proceedings of the National Academy of Scientists* (*PNAS*) from which many of the underlying papers came. The authors have done a good job of simplifying difficult material without dumbing it down, and most readers will find it understandable and interesting.

1. Climate Change and Terrestrial Range Shift

Megan Brittany Smith

Throughout geologic time, life on earth has experienced five previous extinctions that culminated in the disappearance of over 90% of biodiversity on the planet (National Geographic Society 2007). Today, increasing rates of biodiversity loss indicate that earth's sixth extinction is already underway. Its cause has been attributed to several interacting anthropogenic factors such as habitat fragmentation, land degradation, habitat loss, and climate change. Changes in the earth's climate can be broadly observed through an increase in surface temperatures. Over the past 100 years, earth's average surface temperature has increased by approximately 0.74°C and temperatures are only expected to rise as CO_2 and other green house gases concentrations increase in the atmosphere (IPCC Fourth Assessment Report: Climate Change 2007). These changes have directly impacted global species, which have started to shift their geographic distributions toward higher latitudes and elevations in response to rising temperatures (Chen *et al.* 2011).

Abiotic conditions like temperature act as filters that establish species' local community membership by acting on species' functional traits. Climate change will alter these filters with increasing temperatures and therefore will alter the composition of species' communities by selecting for atypical ecological traits belonging to different species more adaptable to the new climate conditions (Sandel and Dangremond 2011). Therefore, species inhabiting warmer weather regimes at lower elevations and latitudes will need to shift their ranges as their weather regime becomes restricted to higher elevations and latitudes to avoid extinction (Ujvari *et al.* 2011). For that reason, vagile, generalist species and competitive, invasive species may come to dominate biological communities if they are favored by new climate regimes and if native, non-vagile, specialists are unable to shift with their ranges.

Studies investigating the importance of European butterfly ecological traits as correlates of extinction risk and distribution change in the face of climate change revealed that non-vagile, habitat specialists and individuals with smaller body sizes will experience distribution declines because they may be incapable of tracking changes within the environment since they are confined to small, isolated habitat patches (Mattila *et al.* 2011). Additionally, research examining how climate change will affect the course of invasion of California's grasses found that increasing temperatures would select for the ecological traits of exotic invasive grass species, thus manipulating the composition of these grassland communities and facilitating the extinction of native species (Sandel and Dangremond 2011).

Interestingly, most of these results are obtained through niche-based modeling techniques that use current species' distributions and ranges and measures of climate variables within these systems to extrapolate species' distributions and ranges under future climate scenarios. However, there may be other factors involved besides climatic variables that influence a species' future range expansion or contraction. For example, a species' evolutionary behavioral patterns could prevent them from tracking environmental changes within their habitats. Within Australia, water pythons' food resources were eradicated from the python's dry-season feeding ranges by an extreme climatic event. However, instead of tracking their prey's new distributions, the pythons remained in their territories and starved to death. Because the pythons tracked their food re-source availability through habitat features rather than prey num-bers, they were unable to adapt to climatic changes within their en-vironment despite their high dispersal ability (Ujvari *et al.* 2011).

Despite these contradictory results, it is undeniable that cli-mate change will decrease the survivability of many species, ulti-mately driving them to extinction and reducing biodiversity world-wide.

Rapid Range Shifts of Species Associated with High Levels of Climate Warming

Changes in climate are impacting biodiversity on a global scale. Recent evidence has suggested that numerous terrestrial species are shifting their geographic ranges to higher elevations and latitudes in response to warming temperatures. However, previous studies have yet to demonstrate a direct link between the warming climate and species' range shifts. Using a combination of data from several studies, Chen *et al.* (2011) analyzed the mean latitude range shifts across species of 23 taxonomic groups per region and the mean ele-vation range shifts across species of 31 taxonomic groups per region. The authors then compared these observed range shifts to expected range shifts necessary for taxonomic groups to remain in the same average temperature zone. The results suggest that the rates of terres-trial range shifts in latitude and elevation are two to three times fast-er than previously described. Additionally, the authors found that the observed latitudinal and elevation range shifts were correlated with the expected range shifts, suggesting a causal relationship be-tween warming temperatures and terrestrial species' range shifts. De-spite these results, there was variation in the directional range shifts among species, indicating that other internal and external factors influence terrestrial species distributions.

Chen *et al.* collected data from previous studies to analyze the current rates of elevation and latitudinal range shifts of terrestrial taxonomic groups. Though other studies investigated the range shifts of individual species, the authors averaged the response of a taxonomic group in a specific region and used this mean as a single observation (i.e. plants in Switzerland). These authors determined range shifts by comparing the differences between two temporally separated recordings of a taxonomic group's range margins (the average of a group's upper/cold and lower/warm temperature range). The latitudinal shift of taxonomic groups was categorized as poleward, stable, or Equatorward while the elevation shift was categorized as up, stable, or down. A figure showing the observed latitudinal shifts of the northern range boundaries of species of four taxonomic groups in Britain was constructed.

The authors extracted regional temperature increases from previous studies or identified the time periods and locations of the regions using CRU_TS2.0 data at 0.5° resolution. They gridded each region and then averaged the temperature across the grid cells to obtain a mean yearly temperature for the area in question. The regional temperature increase over each time period was then obtained by measuring the change in temperature between two temporally separate recordings.

The authors then derived the expected range shifts of the study's taxonomic groups to assess the possible link between the changing climate and terrestrial species' range shifts. Chen *et al.* calculated the expected elevation range shift by first computing the lapse rate, which is the decrease in degrees Celsius per increase in meters. For each region, Chen *et al.* divided the regional temperature increase by the lapse rate to calculate an estimate of the elevation increase or decrease a taxonomic group would have to make to remain within the same temperature range.

Latitudinal range shifts were estimated by first calculating the temperature-distance transfer rate, which is the decrease in degrees Celsius per increase in kilometer of latitude, using CRU_CL2.0 data on a global 10' grid. After gridding each region, the authors identified the nearest cell that was 0.5°C cooler than an original cell. The transfer rate was computed by dividing the temperature difference between the two cells by the latitudinal distance in kilometers between the cells. Then, Chen *et al.* averaged these measurements across every cell in the region to obtain the final transfer rate. The expected latitudinal shifts were determined by dividing the regional temperature increase by its corresponding transfer rate. These shifts represent an estimate of the latitude increase or decrease that a species would need to make to remain in the same temperature range. A figure comparing the observed and expected elevation and latitudinal range shifts for the taxonomic groups was constructed.

The authors found that taxonomic groups shifted their boundaries north of the Equator at a median rate of 16.9 kilometers per decade and that species shifted to higher elevations by a median rate of 11.0 meters per decade. A previous meta-analysis study, which looked at individual species rather than taxonomic groups per region, reported that species' shifts were increasing north of the Equator at a rate of 6.1 kilometers per decade and to higher elevations at a rate of 6.1 meters per decade. Chen *et al.*'s new rates suggests that species' range shifts are moving at a much faster rate, indicating that terrestrial species are responding to climate change more rapidly than previously proposed.

Most significantly, Chen *et al.* found a correlation between the observed range shifts of the taxonomic groups and their expected range shifts. Although other studies suggest that species lag in their response to warming temperatures, nearly equal amounts of taxonomic groups have exceeded expected range shifts as have fallen below in response to climate change. In contrast, the observed distances moved in elevation by species are much shorter than those proposed by the expected range shifts. This may be due to a variety of factors that include difficulty of movement at higher elevations and directional climate complexities found on mountainsides.

Interestingly, although 75% of species moved north, 22% of species shifted southwards in latitude against expectations. Similarly, 25% of species shifted to lower elevations instead of following expected range shifts to higher elevations. *Chen et al.* identified three processes that could account for the diversity of species' range shifts. These processes include time delays in species' responses to climate change, physiological limits, and other interacting drivers of change. For example, some species may lag behind in response to climate change if they specialize in a certain habitat or if they are immobile. Other species may exhibit different responses to increasing temperatures at different stages in their life cycles. Species' ranges may also be determined by non-climatic driving factors such as competition with other species and habitat loss.

Although further studies investigating the physiological, ecological, and environmental drivers of species boundaries are needed to assess the variation in range shifts found in this study, Chen *et al.'s* findings overall suggest that species' ranges are shifting faster than reported and that these range shifts are connected to rising temperatures worldwide.

Ecological Correlates of Distribution Change and Range Shift in Butterflies

Increasing evidence suggests that the worldwide biodiversity loss should be attributed to anthropogenic disturbance, particularly habitat loss and climate change. To conserve biodiversity, scientists must identify the factors driving population decline. The ecological traits of a focal species and the traits of species they interact with have previously been correlated with species' extinction risks and distribution changes. Mattila *et al.* (2011) analyzed the distribution declines (area of occupancy) and range shifts (extent and direction) of 95 threatened and non-threatened butterfly species in Finland to identify ecological traits that influence species' distribution changes and range shifts. These traits included larval specificity, resource distribution, dispersal ability, adult habitat breadth, flight period length, body size, and overwintering stage. The results show that the distribution of Finnish butterflies has declined substantially, with the distribution of threatened species' declining more so than non-threatened species. Additionally, the authors found that the ranges of butterfly species have shifted in both direction and degree, with non-threatened species shifting more so than threatened species. Ecological specialization at the larval or adult stage, as well as poor dispersal ability and large body size, affect both distribution declines and range shifts. These results suggest that highly dispersive generalists will eventually dominate biological communities as result of climate change and habitat fragmentation. However, both non-threatened and threatened species are prone to extinction since both groups possess traits that make them vulnerable to range shifts and distribution declines.

Mattila *et al.* collected Finnish butterfly species data from several scientific papers to assess if threatened and non-threatened species differ in their distribution and range shifts. The authors first categorized the 95 Finland butterfly species as threatened or non-threatened using The Finnish Red List of Species. Butterfly species that were classified as near-threatened, vulnerable, endangered, or critically endangered in the Finnish Red List of Species were classified as by the authors as threatened. The other species were classified as non-threatened.

The authors then determined the distributions, distribution changes, and range shifts of each butterfly species. The distributions were based on the Atlas of Finnish Macrolepidoptera. The distributions are given as the number of occupied 10 km X 10 km grid cells found in the Finnish national coordinate system. The distribution data in the Atlas is categorized into old (before 1988) and new (1988–1997) observations. The authors calculated the distribution changes per butterfly species by finding the difference between the old and new occupied cells, and dividing by the number of old cells.

These values were reported as a negative or positive percent, depending on the direction of the distribution change. Range shifts (the movement of the center of the distribution for each species) were measured by taking the difference between the centers of the distributions between the two timescales (old and new). The range shifts were reported in distance (km) and direction (degrees). A figure displaying the direction of range shifts for non-threatened and threatened species and a table reporting the direction of range shifts for all species were constructed.

Mattila *et al.* then extracted data from previous scientific papers to determine if the ecological characteristics of Finnish butterflies affect distribution changes and range shifts. First, the authors categorized larval host-plant specificity in Finland into three classes: monophages (feed on a single plant species), oligophages (restricted to one genus of food plants), and polyphages (feed on more than one genus). Monophage data were exclusively used to analyze the effects of resource distribution since their food supply is limited. Plant distribution data were collected from the Atlas of the Distribution of Vascular Plants in Finland and was reported as the number of occupied 10-km grid squares in the Finnish national coordinate system.

Butterfly dispersal information was obtained using a previous paper's data. Experienced lepidopterists in Finland received questionnaires and were asked to report the dispersal ability index (on a scale from 0 – 10) for each butterfly species. The 0 value represented an extremely immobile species, while the 10 value represented an extremely mobile species. The questionnaires were averaged to obtain the average dispersal ability for each butterfly species.

Additionally, the authors categorized Finnish butterfly habitats into types: uncultivable lands (edge zones next to industrial areas, harbor and storage areas, loading places, un-cropped fields, and other areas that have been impacted by humans), meadows (noncultivated grasslands), forest edges (roadsides), and bogs. Using these habitat types, Mattila *et al.* formed an index of adult habitat breadth.

This index reports the number of habitat types in which adult butterflies were found. An index value of 1 represents specialist species. Specialist species were confined to one habitat type. An index value of 2 represents intermediate species (those that can inhabit two habitat types), and an index value of 3 represents generalist species. Generalists could occupy three or four habitat types.

The average length of the flight period (days) for each butterfly species was extracted from a previous scientific paper. Wingspan (mm) acted as a measure of butterfly body size because wingspan correlates with body size. Finally, the authors did not include phylogenetic corrections because the information was unavailable, and earlier analyses using preliminary phylogeny showed no change in the results. Two graphs displaying the percent distribution change of species exhibiting larval resource specificity and variation in adult habitat breadth were constructed. Two other graphs demonstrating the effect of body size and dispersal ability on distribution change were also constructed.

Mattila *et al.* analyzed butterfly distribution changes using standard statistical analyses. They conducted two separate analyses for testing the effects of ecological characteristics (larval specificity and habitat breadth) and life history traits (dispersal ability, body size, length of flight period) on distribution changes since data concerning larval specificity and habitat breadth for 14 northern butterfly species could not be found. The authors analyzed range shifts using circular statistics.

The authors found that the distribution of Finnish butterflies declined on average by 35%. Threatened butterfly species' distributions declined by 63%, while non-threatened butterfly species' distributions declined by 26%. The ecological traits driving the distribution declines were larval specificity and adult habitat breadth. In particular, Monophagous butterfly species' distributions declined more than the distributions of oligophages and polyphages. Additionally, the habitat specialists' and intermediate species' distribu-

19

tions declined more than the distributions of habitat generalist species, with the largest decline seen in the habitat specialists. Within the habitat specialists, the distributions of species inhabiting semi-natural meadows and bogs declined more than edge specialists. Life history traits that contributed to distribution declines were dispersal ability and body size.

Mattila *et al.* also found that all butterfly species shifted an average of 22.6 km to the northeast (74.2°). Non-threatened species shifted an average of 30.3 km to the northeast (73.7°), while threatened species only shifted an average of 7.9 km in no consistent direction. The authors asserted that these shifts were caused by changes in climate because Finland's climatic isotherms move to the northeast, near to where the butterfly species seem to be moving. The directions of the range shifts were not influenced by larval specificity or adult habitat breadth. However, they were influenced by dispersal ability, body size, and flight period length. Species that had better dispersal ability, a smaller body size, and a longer flight period experienced larger range shifts in the direction of the overall, average range shift for the butterfly species.

These results indicate that ecological specialization, whether at the larval or adult stage, contributed to Finnish butterfly species' distribution declines and range shifts. Specialist species may be incapable of following changes in the environment (i.e. changes in climate), because these species were isolated and confined to small habitat patches. For example, half of the habitat specialist species lived in semi-natural grasslands or natural bogs. These habitats had consistently declined in area since the 1950s–1960s. Therefore, habitat specialization, combined with poor dispersal ability, contributed to the inability of specialists to shift their ranges. Additionally, most specialist species were categorized as threatened species, which may explain why the threatened species did not shift their ranges to the same degree as non-threatened species. Overall, the results suggest that future biological communities will be dominated by generalist species that are efficient dispersers.

Mattila *et al.*'s findings demonstrate that the ecological traits of Finnish butterfly species influence the distribution changes and range shifts of these species. However, it is imperative to recognize that both threatened and non-threatened species share traits that make them vulnerable to extinction. Therefore, scientists should focus on protecting current, threatened species, as well as species that may be at risk to extinction in the future.

Climate Change and the Invasion of California by Grasses

Abiotic conditions—such as temperature and precipitation—determine local plant community membership by favoring groups with specific functional traits. However, climate change will alter abiotic factors, causing the composition of plant communities to shift by selecting for different functional traits. In some ecosystems, exotic, invasive species may possess functional traits favored by the new climate regime. Therefore, climate change may exacerbate native biodiversity loss by facilitating the spread of invasive species. To determine if climate change will alter the course of invasion of California's already heavily invaded grass flora community, Sandel and Dangremond (2011) evaluated the differences in trait composition of native and exotic species groups and evaluated the contemporary trait-climate relationships across the state. The authors mapped the distributions of all grass species within California and then calculated the mean trait characteristics, mean climate values, and human influence indexes across 800 discrete zones within the state. They found that exotic species were more likely to be annual, taller, with larger leaves, larger seeds, a higher specific leaf area, and a higher leaf nitrogen percentage than native species. These traits were associated with higher temperatures across the entire state, indicating that increasing temperatures caused by climate change will favor traits possessed by exotic species. Ultimately, this may lead to the dominance of exotic species within California's grassland communities.

Sandel and Dangremond mapped the distributions of all grass species within California. The study's maps were based on a map of California that divided the state into 35 floristically defined sub-regions. These sub-regions were divided into 100 m elevation bands using a digital elevation map of California. These divisions resulted in 800 discrete zones across the state. The authors used a flora of California, the Jepson Manual, to determine where grass species occur in each zone. The Jepson Manual was also used to determine whether each species was native or exotic. Exotic species were defined as those that were least naturalized and could be invasive. Particular attention was paid to the species listed by the USDA as invasive and noxious weeds.

The authors collected trait information on the grass species in California. These traits included maximum height, plant lifespan, leaf lifespan, seed mass, month of first flowering, length of flowering period, specific leaf area, leaf length and width, leaf N concentration per mass and per area, and photosynthetic pathway. The data were collected from the Jepson Manual species accounts, published sources such as the Glopnet database, genus-level information, and garden seed information databases. When multiple trait values were available for a species, the authors used the mean of all values. Trait information for species varied from complete to very incomplete. The means for each trait were calculated across all species present in each of the 800 zones. A figure demonstrating trait-based filtering on community membership imposed by climate was constructed, as was a table comparing trait geometric means of exotic and native grass species of California.

The time of introduction for each exotic species was obtained from the California Consortium of Herbaria records, which recorded plant species introductions based on the species first date of collection. The number of exotic species known in a particular year was divided by the percentage of native species that were known for that year to estimate the number of exotic grass species in the state through time.

The authors combined PRISM and Daymet climate data for California to calculate climate variable means for each of the 800 zones. The final set of climate variables obtained were mean annual temperature, seasonality of temperature (annual maximum minus annual minimum temperatures), annual precipitation, potential evapotranspiration, water balance (total precipitation minus PET), months of water deficit (the number of months of the year with PET > precipitation), and cumulative water deficit (summed water deficit in all months of deficit, expressed as negative numbers).

Human impacts on California's ecosystems included increasing the rate of species introductions or producing disturbances that favor exotic species. These possibilities were examined using the Human Influence Index (HII), which measures human impacts by incorporating population density, land cover changes, accessibility, and electrical power infrastructure. The mean HII value was calculated within each of the 800 zones. Both HII and climate variables were treated equally within the study's analysis.

After collecting data, Sandel and Dangremond statistically assessed whether native and exotic species differed in their trait states. The richness of native and exotic species were calculated and then the species richness of each group, as well as the proportion of species in each zone that were exotic, were compared to mean annual temperature and mean annual precipitation. Next, the authors determined how the traits of the grass flora as a whole related to climate by plotting climate variables against zone mean trait values across all 800 zones.

A quantitative prediction for the prevalence of exotic species per zone was calculated based on the relationship between temperature and zone mean trait values for native species, as well as the relationship between species' trait value and the probability that species was native. The authors only used zone mean trait values of native species to avoid predicting the proportion of exotic species from trait means that included exotic species. A loess regression was used to fit a curve to the temperature-trait relationship for native species. Then, a logistic regression was used to estimate the probability that a species with a given trait value was native. When combined, these two regressions allowed the authors to start with a temperature, obtain the predicted zone mean trait value of a zone at that temperature, and to convert this into a prediction of the fraction of the community in that zone that was native. This approach was demonstrated using leaf width in Figure 2.

Since mean zone traits were less variable than individual species traits, the range of predictions for proportion of natives was smaller than the observed range. Therefore, the predicted proportion provided an index of relative susceptibility to exotic species, rather than a 1:1 prediction for the proportion of native species. This index was easily rescaled by using information of the actual proportion of native species within just a few sites. The authors then used further statistical methods to relate the predicted proportion and the actual proportion of native species for five randomly selected sites. They rescaled all predicted proportions according to these results to obtain a properly scaled prediction of the proportion of native species.

Finally, the authors assessed spatial structure in climate and species-level data by separating two sources of climate variation: moving up an elevational gradient within a sub-region, and moving across sub-regions at a constant elevation. Relationships were calculated across all 800 zones, along elevation gradients within each zone, and across sub-regions at a constant elevation.

Sandel and Dangremond found that grass species richness varied across the state, with a maximum of 163 and minimum of 3 species in a zone. The proportion of exotic grass species within a zone varied between 0% and 66% within zones. Native species richness showed a hump-shaped relationship with temperature while the proportion of species that were exotic increased strongly with temperature. Mean annual precipitation was not strongly related to the richness or the proportion of exotic species. A map displaying the patterns of species richness of grass in California was constructed, as was a map displaying the proportion of species within a zone that were exotic. Additionally, figures displaying the relationship of species richness and climate were constructed.

There was a total of 258 native and 177 exotic grass species in California. These two groups differed significantly in their traits. Exotic species were more likely to be annual, taller, have longer and wider leaves, a higher specific leaf area, a higher leaf N percentage, and a higher seed mass. Noxious invasive weeds had the most extreme trait values, while most exotic species were intermediate between weeds and native species. Many of these traits were strongly related to mean annual temperature. At warmer sites, species were larger (taller and larger-leaved), with a higher specific leaf area, a greater leaf N percentage and mass, shorter-lived leaves, larger seeds, earlier flowering times, and longer flowering seasons. The proportion of grass perennial species decreased with increasing temperatures as well. Figures displaying the relationship of temperature and grass traits were constructed, as was a table displaying the statistical results of comparisons of climate variables and zone mean traits.

The authors also found that with increasing cumulative water deficits, decreasing water balances, and increasing months at water deficit, grasses became longer-leaved with a higher specific leaf area, a higher N leaf percentage and mass, and with larger leaves. As human impacts increased, zones became exotic-like in their trait composition, revealing the increased richness of exotic species in heavily used areas.

Additionally, the results showed that an increase in elevational gradients within sub-regions led to reductions in grass mean height. However, there was little relationship between height and temperature when elevation was constant. Seed mass showed both positive and negative relationships to temperature within sub-regions. At low elevations (across sub-regions) seed mass increased with temperature, while at high elevation, it decreased. Figures displaying the relationships between mean annual temperature and these two traits were constructed.

Sandel and Dangremond predicted the proportion of species in each zone that were native using only zone mean annual temperature, trait-temperature relationships for native species, and trait differences between native and exotic species groups. Using leaf width patterns, they found that the proportion of native species was strongly correlated with the observed proportion. However, the relationship was nonlinear and the predicted proportions covered a smaller range of values than the observed proportions, causing a poor fit to the 1:1 line. The authors rescaled the predicated proportions based on five randomly sampled sites where the proportion of native species was known. This led to quantitative and accurate predictions of the proportion of native species. A figure displaying the corrected prediction for the proportion of species that were native was constructed.

Finally, the authors found that prior to 1860, there were 20–30 exotic species established in California. This number increased sharply through the 1900s. The continued arrival of exotic species into California significantly changed the composition of the exotic flora. California's exotic flora became more perennial, more C_4, and larger-seeded over time. Figures displaying the changes in the exotic grass flora of California over time were constructed.

Overall, two conditions must be met for climate change to favor one species group (exotic grass) over another (native grasses). The changing climate (an increase in California's mean annual temperature) must alter filters that act on plant functional traits, leading to communities with altered trait compositions. The two groups must also differ along trait axes. Both these conditions were met in California.

The present distribution of grass species richness within California already show that the proportion of species within a zone that were exotic and the proportion that were noxious weeds were strongly and positively related to mean annual temperature. However, since exotic species were taller and had more light-capturing ability than native species, they may outcompete natives for light. The larger seeds of exotic species also could give them a competitive advantage at the seedling stage. Additionally, increasing temperatures favored traits for which exotics had higher mean values than natives. Therefore, exotic and invasive species may come to dominate California's grassland community since current noninvasive exotics could become invasive as temperatures increase within the state over time.

Disproportional Risk for Habitat Loss of High-Altitude Endemic Species Under Climate Change

Scientists project that climate change will alter the distributions and range shifts of biota, ultimately causing an increase in terrestrial species' extinction rates. In many mountainous areas, warming temperatures have already generated an upward shift of tree lines. Therefore, range-restricted, high-altitude, endemic species inhabiting mountain ranges are particularly at risk since the upward shift of the tree line may significantly reduce these endemic species' habitat areas. Using a Potential Climate Tree Line (PCT) model and statistical analyses, Dirnbock *et al.* (2011) analyzed the loss of available habitats for high-altitude endemics of five Austrian Alps taxonomic groups (vascular plants, snails, spiders, butterflies, and beetles). Habitat loss was attributed to the upward shift of forest species. Additionally, the authors investigated whether hotspots of endemics would be disproportionally affected by habitat loss. Dirnbock *et al.* found that even under the weakest climate change scenario (+1.8°C by 2100), above tree line area was reduced by 77%. The results also demonstrated that areas with high endemic species richness showed the largest losses of suitable habitat. Therefore, endemic species richness was positively related to above tree line area loss. These results suggest that endemic hotspots in the Alps will be disproportionally affected by habitat loss caused by climate change induced forest expansion. Combined with these species' range restrictions, their ability to persist in the face of climate change may be greatly reduced.

The authors conducted their study in Austria, a landlocked country in Central Europe. The mountains of the eastern Alps cover two-thirds of Austria, and during the Pleistocene, approximately 70% of them were glaciated. These glaciations led to the widespread migrations, range restrictions, and survival of species in isolated refugia located in non-glaciated, flat, low, peripheral mountains. This process led to the evolution and speciation of different lineages and taxa. Many endemics are currently restricted to the northeast peripheral mountains of the Alps due to their limited migration ability.

Dirnbock *et al.* used data from an Austrian endemic species inventory that reported each species' distribution (presence/absence) in grid cells encompassing a 35-km^2 area. They selected taxonomic groups containing a high number of endemic species with ranges primarily in Austria and whose habitats were restricted to areas above the current tree line suitable for forest growth. Species were excluded if they were restricted to habitats incapable of forest colonization, either due to the absence of topsoil or the presence of high levels of disturbance (rock habitats, screes). Of the 177 high altitude endemics, 134 species occupied habitat above the tree line that was suitable for forest growth and these 134 species were used in the study. This group was composed of 45% beetles, 32% vascular plants, 10% spiders, 9% butterflies, and 4% snails.

Since both climate and land use changes trigger the upward shift of the tree line, the authors used a potential climate tree line (PCT) Model to isolate climate as the contributing factor driving forest expansion. Dirnbock *et al.* derived the current regional tree line by overlaying Austrian forest distribution on a digital elevation model (DEM) in geographic information systems (GIS) computer program. Since different tree species respond individually to climatic variables, the authors divided Austria into nine forest regions based on species. The precipitation sum and monthly mean temperature from April to September were sampled randomly in each region along the tree line. These variables acted as drivers of tree line location within the model. Edaphic traits and ecosystem disturbances were excluded from the model.

Once constructed, the authors used the PCT model to test five climate scenarios to determine how climate change will drive loss of area above the tree line. These standard IPCC scenarios included B1 (an increase of 1.8°C, the minimum expected projected temperature for 2100), A1T and B2 (an increase in 2.4°C), A1B (an increase of 2.8°C), A2 (an increase of 3.4°C), and A1FI (an increase of 4°C). Dirnbock *et al.* next calculated the proportional loss of area above the tree line by assigning the current area under the PCT model a value of 100%. Therefore, if the model computed a value of 1, the region experienced a complete loss of area above the tree line. A value of 0 indicated no change in area above the tree line.

A statistical test was used to determine if loss of area above the tree line was higher in cells that contained at least one endemic species compared to those that contained none. Dirnbock *et al.* used an alternative statistical test to assess if endemic species richness and altitude predicted loss of area above the tree line.

They found that with minimum expected climate change (an increase in 1.8°C) a 77% loss of above tree line area due to tree line expansion resulted. Under maximum expected climate change (an increase in 4°C), the hotspots of high altitude endemism were restricted to a few fragmented mountaintops. Interestingly, the results also suggest that areas containing endemic species will not loose more above tree line terrain than areas lacking endemic species.

Maps comparing the number of endemic species, the proportional loss of area above the tree line by 2100, and the proportional loss of area above the tree line under two other climate scenarios were constructed.

Additionally, Dirnbock *et al.* determined that grid cells with low to intermediate endemic species richness (1–8 endemic species) showed small losses in above tree line area. In contrast, grid cells with high endemic species richness (9–30 endemic species) showed the largest losses in above tree line area. When the authors pooled endemic species richness across all five taxonomic groups, they found that species richness was positively related to the loss of above tree line area. The same results were found for species richness within three of the five taxonomic groups (vascular plants, beetles, and snails). Although an increase in altitude resulted in a decrease in species richness, Dirnbock *et al.* established that endemic species richness was related to loss of above tree line area independent of altitude. Individual analyses of each taxonomic group revealed that beetles' and snails' habitat showed a disproportionate above tree line area loss while spiders and butterflies demonstrated the opposite results. A figure comparing the number of endemic species to the proportional loss of above tree line area for each climate scenario was constructed, as was a separate table recording the loss of area above the tree line for each climate scenario and for different groups of endemic species.

Dirnbock *et al.*'s results suggest that endemic species' hotspots in the Alps will be affected by habitat loss generated by climate change-driven forest expansion. In particular, these hotspots will be affected by forest expansion more so than regions with low species richness. Hotspots of endemism within the Alps are located predominately on flat mountain plateaus that rise slightly above the tree line. Therefore, endemic species' suitable habitats are limited to begin with, ultimately leaving little to no available habitat when forests expand slightly into their territory.

Forest expansion did not affect spiders' and butterflies' habitats because these species' also inhabit the higher, central mountain ranges of the Alps, thus alleviating their climate induced extinction risk from habitat loss. Spiders and butterflies also have a higher dispersal capability due to the presence of mobile adults (butterflies, ballooning spiders). Therefore, these species could have re-colonized several larger regions in the Alps after the glacial period ended.

Overall, a species' risk of extinction in future climate change scenarios corresponds with its ability to shift with its suitable habitats. Yet, as climate change drives the upward expansion of the tree line on mountainsides, non-forested mountaintops will become increasingly fragmented. This fragmentation will not only reduce endemic high-altitude species' available habitat, but it will also obstruct the lateral movement of these species. Since many endemics are poor dispersers and habitat specialists, the migration capacity of these species' will be greatly reduced.

On the Generality of a Climate-Mediated Shift in the Distribution of the American Pika (*Ochotona princeps*)

Alpine species are extremely vulnerable to climate change-induced extinctions due to their physiological and geographic constraints. Scientists have already documented climate change-generated population extirpations and distributional shifts for numerous alpine plant and mammal species, such as the American pika (*Ochotona princeps*). However, few studies have investigated the specific climatic drivers that cause these local species' extinction at lower alpine levels. Using models and surveys of 69 American Pika population sites, Erb *et al.* (2011) analyzed pika distribution change throughout the Southern Rocky Mountains by assessing the effects of landscape, microhabitat, and climatic factors on pika persistence. Elevation, maximum summer temperature, annual precipitation, and habitat characteristics with potential climate-buffering effects (talus depth, porosity of rocks, soil moisture, and rock type) acted as the predictor variables. The authors found that only 4 of the 69 pika populations were extirpated in the Southern Rockies. However, these four sites revealed that climatic factors, rather than habitat features, determined pika persistence. Additionally, these 4 sites were among the driest pika habitats in the region; they lacked a sub-talus water source and experienced a smaller mean annual precipitation in comparison to other pika sites. These results suggest that water, in the form of precipitation and sub-surface moisture, was the primary driver of pika distribution patterns in the study region. Therefore, increased drying trends could put American pika populations at risk to climate change-induced extinction.

The authors conducted their research at 69 sites historically occupied by pikas in the Southern Rocky Mountains of southern Wyoming, Colorado, and New Mexico. The sites were defined as those with recorded pika presence before 1980—the year when climate change became prominent in datasets. The dates of the historical records varied from 1872 to 1979, and the sites were also chosen based on geographic accuracy. The data were collected from 800 historical records of pika presence found in museum records, literature sources, and georeferenced museum specimens. Climate data for each site was accumulated between 1908 and 2007. Site elevation varied from 2703 to 4340 m and the most common vegetation at the sites consisted of alpine forbs, grasses, willow, conifers, and aspen.

The authors sent out crews to each of the 69 sites to assess current pika occupancy. The crews searched for signs of pika presence by detecting individual organisms through sight and sound and by identifying fresh pika food stores (haypiles). If signs of pika occupancy were not found, crews returned 3–5 months later and searched the sites extensively within a 3 kilometer (km) radius. A minimum of 0.5 hours was spent per hectare searching talus for signs of pika presence. While at each site, the crews collected data on microhabitat features. A map of the 69 sites historically occupied by the American pika, differentiated by recent occupancy status, was constructed.

Erb *et al.* then compared models of pika persistence that incorporated elevation, maximum summer temperature, annual precipitation, and site characteristics with potential climate buttering effects (rock type, talus depth, porosity of individual rocks, and evidence of persistent soil moisture beneath the talus) to assess landscape, microhabitat, and climate characteristics as possible drivers of pika population extirpation. The authors' model comparisons were guided by pika persistence hypotheses and results from previous studies. The models represented the following hypotheses: 1) pikas persist in locations where the least change in climate (temperature and precipitation) has occurred; 2) pikas persist in areas where the climate has predominantly been wet and cool; 3) pikas persist in sites where they have been exposed to the least climatic variability; 4) pikas persist in locations with the deepest talus, most porous and insulating rock, and where water or ice persist under the talus; 5) pikas persist at higher elevation locations. A table displaying the hypotheses and the candidate model covariates was constructed.

The authors found that only 4 of the 69 pika population sites in the Southern Rockies lacked recent signs of *O. princeps* in 2008. However, the pattern of these extirpation sites reveal that pika persistence was best explained by water, in the form of mean precipitation and the persistence of moisture under the talus. These four sites were the driest of the 69 sites within the Southern Rockies. The mean annual precipitation across all sites between 1908 and 2007 was 884 mm and the mean annual precipitation across extirpation sites was 593 mm. The four sites also lacked a sub-talus water source. Overall, these results support the authors' second and fourth hypotheses. A graph displaying observed and predicted pika occupancy as a function of local mean precipitation, change in precipitation, and presence of sub-talus water was constructed, as was a figure comparing observed pika occupancy with mean annual precipitation between 1908 and 2007.

The extirpation locations did not experience significant climate variability. There was very little change in precipitation levels at the extirpation locations since 1980. Therefore, summer maximum temperatures, change in summer maximum temperatures, and variation in both summer maximum and annual precipitation did not support pika persistence. Additionally, elevation, talus depth, and rock porosity did not predict pika persistence. A figure comparing observed pika occupancy with change in mean annual precipitation between the years of 1908 and 1979 and 1980 and 2007 was constructed.

In contrast, Erb *et al.* found that since 1980, maximum summer temperatures across all sites have averaged 0.48°C warmer than they were from 1908 to 1979. Changes in maximum temperature varied among sites (−1.2°C to +2.5°C), as did changes in annual precipitation (−80 mm to +203 mm, −8.0% to +24.1%). The overall trend in the study region demonstrated an increase in annual precipitation across all sites (+46 mm, +5.6%). These results demonstrate that the overall pika population sites experienced climatic change even though the 4 extirpation sites did not.

Although low precipitation and sub-talus moisture drove pika extinction in the Southern Rockies, pika population sites experiencing a decrease in annual precipitation were not more vulnerable to extirpation. This may seem contradictory with the authors' previous findings; however, the sites that experienced a decrease in precipitation since 1980 were previously among the wettest locations within the study region. Although these 13 drying sites did not significantly differ in mean post 1980 precipitation levels from the other 56 sites, it would nevertheless be important to monitor their moisture levels since continued drying trends could place these pika populations at risk to extirpation in the near future.

Additionally, though the four extirpation sites were the driest within the study region, pika occupancy was detected at these locations within the past century. Erb *et al.* proposed that these sites may have been marginal habitats that required immigration from adjacent populations to maintain their own populations. Therefore, these locations only supported pika populations when climatic conditions facilitated their re-colonization by individuals from nearby sites. Each extinction site experienced a year in which annual precipitation was above the site's upper 99% Confidence Interval 1–4 years before the site's recorded pika presence. This suggests that variable high precipitation conditions facilitated pika dispersal.

The authors also suggested that the dry extirpation sites were unable to support pika populations because they lacked snow cover. The low precipitation levels recorded at these sites resulted in the low accumulation of snow cover. Since snow cover insulates pika populations from extreme cold weather events, the low levels of snow were inefficient to protect the pika populations from low alpine temperatures. Therefore, projected declines in snowpack throughout the western United States indicate that pika habitats in regions like the Southern Rockies may soon experience drier conditions, placing further pika populations at risk to climate change induced extinction.

Gray-Brown Mouse Lemurs (*Microcebus griseorufus*) as an Example of Distributional Constraints through Increasing Desertification

Anthropogenic climate change may threaten endemic species commonly found in biodiversity hotspots around the world. One endemic species of particular concern is the Gray-brown mouse lemur (*Microcebus griseorufus*), a primate species found in Madagascar—a biodiversity hotspot. Currently, climate change is increasing rates of aridity and desertification within the lemurs' habitats. These climatic changes may affect the species' end-of-the-wet-season food supply, an important resource that primarily contributes to their survival during the harsh, dry season. Therefore, to assess the impacts of aridity on lemurs and to identify factors that could inhibit the species' distribution and range expansion under dry conditions, Bohr *et al.* (2011) compared two populations of lemurs in adjacent habitats that differed in humidity levels. They measured differences in lemur abundance, body mass, body condition, and food type abundance between the two sites, and also determined lemur distributions and feeding patterns. The authors found that the more humid site produced more high-quality food and maintained a higher population density of *M. griseorufus,* with individuals in better condition compared to the drier site. The results showed that at the end of the wet season, the lemurs adjusted their home range size to local food plant density, indicating that lemurs modify their food intake at the end of the wet season to prepare for the dry season. A negative, exponential relationship between food plant density and home range size also demonstrated that lemurs had an upper limit for the size of their home ranges. Therefore, primates from the drier habitat were unable to compensate for their reduced food availability by expanding their home range beyond this upper limit. Unfortunately, although lemurs would have the ability to migrate to mesic habitats under drier climate scenarios in search of food, habitat fragmentation in Madagascar could significantly reduce the lemurs' ability to do so.

   M. griseorufus occured in southwestern Madagascar and occupied all vegetation formations from spiny bush to evergreen humid forest. They were the only mouse lemurs that inhabited the driest of these habitats (the spiny bush), and therefore represented the arid end of the genus' ecological niche. In the more mesic parts of its range, it lived with *M. murinus,* and these two species often hybridized. There were distinct dry and wet seasons within the species' habitat, and *M. griseorufus* tended to reduce their day range and activity (and therefore reduce their metabolic rate) during the dry season in response to food shortage. Therefore, lemur energy reserves accumulated during the wet season were crucial for their survival during the dry season.

The study site was located in the Parc National de Tsimanampetsotsa, which experienced highly seasonal rainfall. Recently, this region experienced a shift in maximum rainfall from December and February to March and April. This zone had the highest levels of plant endemism on the island (48% of the genera and 95% of the species were endemic). The majority of the vegetation was xerophytic and was classified among Madagascar's spiny forest formations. There were two different vegetation formations within the study site that varied according to the underlying soil and the soil's water holding capacity. The first location was a dry forest on unconsolidated sands (DFS) and the second location was a spiny bush formation on calcareous soil (XBC). The DFS site was more humid than the XBC site. The study period lasted from April until July 2008. April and May were defined as the late wet season and June and July were defined as the early dry season. A map of the study site showing the different vegetation types and the location of both study plots was displayed.

Within each vegetation structure, the authors established one study plot of 6 ha (150 X 400 m) and placed 96 Sherman Livetraps at 25 m intervals in each plot. Traps were placed 0.5–2.0 m high in the vegetation and were baited with bananas. One trapping session was conducted in each habitat in each season and lasted for 4 consecutive nights. This resulted in a total of 384 trap nights per habitat per season. Captured lemurs were anesthetized and marked with a microchip. They were weighed and their tail circumference was measured at the tail base. In addition to body mass, tail circumference represented body condition since gray-brown mouse lemurs store fat in their tail before the dry season.

Twenty-two individuals (DFS: 6 females, 5 males; XBC: 5 females, 6 males) were supplied with radio collars to assess feeding and ranging patterns. The authors studied feeding behavior through focal observations of 2 radio-collared individuals (1 female, 1 male) per habitat per season. The type of food ingested and the lemur's position each time it moved was recorded. Frequency of feeding on certain food categories was documented rather than time spent feeding on items since the animals time processing and handling food items (fruits, gum, and arthrpods) varied depending on the type of food consumed. All 22 mouse lemurs were sequentially tracked over a total of 8 half-nights by triangulation to assess their spatial and temporal distribution. Home range sizes were estimated using Animal Movement and the minimum-convex-polygon method. The authors compared the sizes of home ranges to test for seasonal variation in home range size between the wet and dry season. Home range data was also analyzed to test for habitat effects. Two graphs displaying the correlations between the numbers of food plants per ha and home range size (ha) for the wet and dry seasons were constructed.

All known food plants within the study plots were mapped using ArcView 3.2a. The plant data were overlaid over home range polygons to assess food availability within the individual home ranges. Food plants that had a height >1 m or a diameter at breast height >10 cm were included in the study. The researchers checked the plants for flowers and fruits twice a month. A graph displaying the phenology of fruit plants in the studied habitats between March and July 2008 was constructed. All the data were assessed using statistical analyses. Three tables displaying the results of the statistical analyses were constructed.

Bohr *et al.* found that the population density in the mesic dry forest was 3 times higher than in the drier spiny bush and that at the end of the wet season, mouse lemurs had higher body masses and larger tail circumferences (fat storage) than at the beginning of the dry season. Lemurs from the dry forest were in better condition than those from the spiny bush. Home ranges were also larger at the end of the wet season than during the dry season. Home range sizes did not differ between the two sites, and home range size was positively correlated with tail circumference.

At the end of the rainy season, observed lemurs fed equally on fruits and gum. However, at the beginning of the dry season, the lemurs ingested more gum over fruits. In the dry forest, lemurs consumed gum and fruits equally, whereas lemurs in the spiny bush primarily consumed gum. Arthropods were also eaten more frequently in the spiny bush than in the dry forest. Tables displaying the diet of *M. griseorufus* in the DFS and the XBC sites, as well as during the wet and dry seasons, were constructed.

Throughout the entire study, the number of fruit-bearing plants was lower and declined faster in the arid spiny bush versus the mesic dry forest. Overall food abundance was high in March, but steadily declined in June and July. A higher total number of fruit-producing versus gum-producing plant individuals were found in the home ranges of the dry forest, and home ranges in the spiny bush had a significantly lower density of fruit-producing plants. The density of gum-producing plants did not differ between sites. Home range size and food plant density correlated negatively at the end of the wet season, indicating that home range size would need to increase exponentially if food abundance was to further decrease. No such relationship was observed during the dry season.

These results demonstrate that there were substantial differences in habitat quality between the two sites, and that the dry forest was the more favorable habitat for *M. griseorufus* since it contained a larger density of the lemurs' favored food: fruit. Lemurs' distribution was therefore linked to food abundance at the end of the wet season, but not during the dry season. The lemurs prepared for the less favorable dry season at the end of the wet season by expanding their home range size and increasing their food intake. They then reduced their metabolic rates and lowered their energy expenses instead of attempting to increase their energy intake. This suggests that the species was limited by bottom-up factors (food resources) rather than top-down factors (predation).

The observed higher population density in the dry forest, with its higher availability of fruit plants, also suggests that the lemur populations were regulated by bottom-up factors (food resources). The lemurs preferred fruit to gum, and arthropods were hunted opportunistically since they were more difficult to locate and defend. Although gum contained concentrations of protein or carbohydrates that exceeded those found in Madagascar fruit, the fruit may have been preferred over gum because the gum contained secondary compounds that inhibit digestion.

The lower density and poorer body condition of the lemurs within the spiny bush indicate that the spiny bush habitat was less favorable than the dry forest habitat. This suggests that the higher proportion of gum-producing plants in the spiny forest could not compensate for the reduced amount of fruit plants at this site. Animals with larger home ranges accumulated more fat in preparation for the dry season. However, if the lemurs were able to extend their home ranges beyond their present sizes, larger home ranges would have been observed in the spiny bush. Clearly, these lemurs were unable to extend their home ranges to include more food resources even when faced with a drier climate and unfavorable food. The animals could have reached a point where home range extension (as compensation for declining food abundance) became unprofitable. Since climate change induced-desiccation will shift food resources toward gum at the expense of fruits, lemurs will need to migrate to more mesic areas to obtain required food resources.

Since *M. griseorufus* inhabits the dry limit of its ecological niche in the xerophytic spiny bush, it will have to migrate to more mesic areas as climate change-induced desiccation shifts its food resources towards unfavorable gum. However, connectivity between habitats in Madagascar has been extensively disrupted by anthropogenic habitat fragmentation. Therefore, conservation efforts must be made to establish connectivity between lemur habitats.

Breeding Success at the Range Margin of a Desert Species: Implications for a Climate-Induced Elevational Shift

Species are limited to specific geographic area by historical contingency and an interaction between extrinsic abiotic and biotic factors and intrinsic dispersal abilities and adaptive traits. Species-occupied areas immediately adjacent to species-absent territories are defined as range margins, which often are associated with poor quality habitat and declining species fitness (reproductive success) and therefore a lower population density. However, if limiting environmental conditions change at a range margin, the distributions of species may expand or retract in response to that change. Hargrove and Rotenberry 2011 investigated whether the breeding success and the abundance of the desert species *Amphispiza bilineata,* the black-throated sparrow, was reduced at its range margins and if these reductions were linked to a potential climate-induced elevational shift. The authors compared the abundance and breeding success (at the nest level, territory level, and population level) of *A. bilineata* at two spatially separate sites over a period of three years. The first site was a mesic environment (characterized by chapparal vegetation) within the sparrow's upper elevation margin. It was located near site two, a desert habitat (characterized by desert scrub vegetation) at lower elevations that was more commonly occupied by the sparrow. The results show that although sparrow abundance was greater at the drier site, the species' reproductive success at the mesic site significantly outperformed the reproductive success of the sparrows inhabiting the drier site during the two driest years of the study. However, the reproductive success of the birds inhabiting the desert scrub environment improved during a year with higher precipitation levels. Despite these observations, there was little indication of an upward elevational shift in the sparrows' distribution over a 26-year period although a warming trend and drier conditions were observed, suggesting the presence of an "ecological trap" within the system. Ultimately, this "ecological trap" could prevent or delay sparrow climate-induced range shifts.

The black-throated sparrow (*A. bilineata*) breeds territorially throughout the desert of the southwest United States and northern Mexico. It is non-territorial in winter. The study area was located at the species' western range margin in San Diego County, California. There, the Peninsular Mountains create a rain barrier to the eastern Colorado Desert. There is a strong ecological gradient that varies with elevation along the eastern slopes of these mountains. This ecological gradient is also correlated with temperature and precipitation. Within this area, the sparrows are abundant in desert habitat east of the Peninsular Mountains but are rare or absent at higher elevations and coastal areas. The species' distributional margin occurs along a plant community transition at mid-elevation between desert scrub and chaparral.

Large-scale sparrow distributions and abundance were calculated using point counts at 90 locations along the full elevational gradient (150–1850 m in elevation over a distance of 30 km) from desert scrub to chaparral vegetation. Point counts lasting 15 minutes were conducted between the 2005–2008 breeding seasons. They were repeated 2–3 times a year using distance sampling with a single observer. The relationship between mean birds per point count and elevation was compared using statistical analysis. Local-scale bird abundance and breeding activity was recorded by establishing 10 study sites along the margin of the sparrows' distribution limits at 1150–1450 m and 6 study sites in lower-elevation desert scrub at 150–650 m. The higher elevation sites were characterized by chaparral vegetation while the lower elevation sites were characterized by desert scrub. Mean distance between the desert scrub and chaparral sites was 13 km, while mean within-habitat distance of sites was 6.7 km. The study sites were approximately 24 ha in area (1200 X 200 m). Local-scale bird abundance was estimated based on territory density estimates at each of the 16 sites using weekly territory mapping during the breeding seasons. The locations of birds and their behaviors were plotted weekly and territories were identifiable based on male singing and aggressive interactions exhibited with neighbors and pairs that foraged closely together. Territory density was calculated for each study site as the maximum number of territories at any point in time. A territory was defined by the presence of a single male during three consecutive weeks. Differences between desert scrub and chaparral sites were tested using a statistical analysis.

Breeding success was calculated by conducting weekly censuses and nest monitoring at each of the 16 study sites during the breeding seasons of 2005–2008. Breeding activity was monitored for each territory from vantage points that were unlikely to cause disturbance. The locations and numbers of all adults and fledglings were mapped weekly at each study site, and all nesting activity was monitored. Survival probability was estimated daily through nest checks. Nests were avoided if they were being constructed or if sparrows were laying eggs. Clutch size and final nest outcome were estimated if possible. Additionally, the authors calculated an index of relative productivity using the fledgling ratio (proportion of total fledglings relative to adults across the season) based on weekly observations of adult and fledgling numbers. Fledglings were identified through begging calls and by visually observing their limited movement. Tail length and mobility were used to approximate fledgling age. Differences in fledgling ratios between desert scrub and chaparral sites were tested using statistical analyses.

A site-specific breeding index was generated by scoring each territory based on the highest stage of progression observed during the breeding season: 1) territorial male alone, 2) adult pair, 3) nest construction, 4) nest with eggs, 5) nest with nestlings, 6) fledglings, and 7) fledglings plus a second nest attempted. Differences in territory breeding index scores were tested using a statistical analysis. Mean clutch size was estimated using nests for which the final clutch size was determined with certainty. Daily nest survival probability was estimated using nests for which the final outcome was known. A maximum-likelihood estimate of daily nest survival probability for each habitat type and year assuming constant daily survival rate was generated using Program MARK, version 5.1. Differences between the two vegetation sites for clutch size and daily nest survival probability were tested using statistical analyses.

The authors used weather data from PRISM Group, Oregon State University to create an approximation of environmental conditions during the study period. This data was compared to 40-year means. The cumulative precipitation during the July to June rain-year, and the mean monthly minimum and maximum temperatures during spring months (March to June, when nesting occurred) were calculated for each site.

Hargrove and Rotenberry found that between 2006 and 2008, the mean monthly maximum temperature during the spring season was 16.2°C greater at the lower-elevation desert scrub sites compared to the higher-elevation chaparral sites, and that the mean minimum temperature was 8.5°C greater at the desert scrubs sites. Over a period of 40 years, the mean monthly maximum temperature in spring increased 2.4°C at the low-elevation desert scrub sties and 2.7°C at the higher-elevation chaparral sites while the mean monthly minimum temperature in spring increased 0.4°C at the low elevation desert scrub sites and 2.1°C at the higher elevation sites. Precipitation levels were lower at the low-elevation desert scrub sites in comparison to the higher-elevation scrub sites. Across the three years of the study, the desert scrub sites experienced 79% less precipitation than the chaparral sites. All the sites and years between 2006 and 2008 were below the 40-year precipitation means. In 2007, the area experienced record drought conditions while 2008 came close to the 40-year mean precipitation levels. A figure displaying the cumulative precipitation during July to June rain-year at desert scrub sites and chaparral sites between 2006 and 2008 was constructed.

The authors also found that mean black-throated sparrow abundance declined toward the upper elevation margin across all three years of the study. Overall abundance was 157% greater in the 150–650 m elevation range (desert scrub sites) than in the 1150–1450 m elevation range (chaparral sites). Sparrows were absent from the 1450–1850 m elevation range. Similarly, territory density between 2006 and 2008 was 81% greater at desert scrub sites than at chaparral sites. A figure displaying the mean black-throated sparrow abundance along the elevation gradient was constructed.

The results show that productivity (ratio of fledglings) was greater at the chaparral study sites across all three years. The most productive year was 2008 followed by 2006, with 2007 being the least productive year. No fledglings were observed at the desert scrub sites in 2006 or 2007, demonstrating a 100% reproductive failure at these sites during the two driest years of the study despite the greater density of birds found at these sites. However, in 2008 (the wetter year), the fledgling ratio was equivalent to the fledgling ratio found at the chaparral sites in 2008. Breeding success measured at the territory level was significantly lower at desert scrub sites than at chaparral sites between 2006 and 2008. The breeding index three-year average at chaparral sites was 4.0 while the breeding index in 2006 and 2007 for the desert scrub sites were 2.4 and 2.0, but was 5.1 in 2008. There were a small number of nests at the desert scrub sites in 2006 and 2007. Although clutch size and daily survival probability could not be estimated in 2007 for desert scrub sites, the authors proposed that the overall pattern was similar to other breeding success measures, suggesting a reduction in both clutch size and nest survival probability at desert scrub sites in the two driest years (2006 and 2007). A reversal of that pattern was seen in 2008. Clutch size was greater at chaparral sites than at desert scrub sites in 2006, but there was no difference between sites in 2008. Lay dates were earlier at desert scrub sites than at chaparral sites. A figure displaying the territory-level breeding success of black-throated sparrows at deserts scrub and chaparral sites between 2006 and 2008 was constructed.

Within southern California, the desert regions are predicted to become warmer and drier within the next 100 years while events such as floods and droughts are expected to increase. Therefore, if the sparrows breeding success improves at the distribution margin, breeding distributions are expected to expand unless there are other fitness-related factors interacting within the system. However, although sparrow-breeding success was greater at the upper elevational margin (since drought was the probable cause of reduced reproduction at the desert scrub sites), the birds showed little sign of any upward shift in their elevation distribution. Higher sparrow abundance persisted at the desert scrub sites even during the direst years of the study and the upper elevational limit did not experience a shift either. The authors additionally did not find evidence for an upward elevational shift for the sparrows at another site despite strong warming trends and drier conditions.

Hargrove and Rotenberry proposed that the sparrows' observed stasis could be attributed to tradeoffs—such as increased survival rates at lower elevations—that increase overall species fitness within the desert scrub habitat. Additionally, the life-history strategy of the sparrow may explain its range stasis. For example, the sparrow species could take advantage of wet years for reproduction while reproductively stagnating during dry years. Finally, desert scrub habitat may have a greater suitability historically for the black-throated sparrows, indicating that the species has evolved a preference for desert scrub vegetation over that of chaparral. Therefore, the greater density of sparrows at sites with reduced reproductive success that are close to sites with lower density and greater reproductive success signals the presence of an ecological trap for this species. Ecological traps can drive a population to extinction and occur when low-quality habitat is preferred over high quality available habitat. So, even if marginal areas have greater climatic suitability, sparrows may still retain an inherited preference for less-suitable central habitat, leading to their extinction. Ultimately, the local biotic interactions of these sparrows outweigh the effects of climate change, thereby inhibiting range shifts.

How well do Predators Adjust to Climate-Mediated Shifts in Prey Distribution? A Study on Australian Water Pythons

The spatial relocation of many species' vital resources has been attributed to climate change. These resources are often other terrestrial prey species. Therefore, predatory species' resilience and survival in the face of climate change depends on their ability to shift their activities away from unsuitable territories to the new ranges their prey inhabits. Ujvari *et al.* (2011) monitored two spatially separate groups of Northern Australian water pythons (*Liasis fuscus*) that were tracking the movements of their primary prey, the dusky rat (*Rattus colletti*), during the wet season. One population of pythons inhabited an area (Beatrice Hill) that contained a large population of rats. The second group of pythons inhabited Fogg Dam, an area that had recently experienced a crash in rat numbers due to a severe flood. The authors measured the population size, the survival rate, and the residual body mass (RBM) of both python groups and found that food (rat) availability was correlated with python RBM. Therefore, the pythons' lower RBM at Fogg Dam was attributed to limited prey availability. As a result, the population's survival rate and size were greatly reduced through starvation, despite the presence of a close, large population of rats at Beatrice Hill. These results suggest that python migrations were signaled by habitat features that indicate prey availability—a life strategy that could inhibit the adaption of pythons to climate induced prey range shifts.

Ujvari *et al.* conducted their study in the Adelaide River floodplain, which lies in the Northern Territory of Australia within the "wet-dry" tropics (131°18'48.19"E, 12°34'14.81"S). The Adelaide River floodplain is a flat, treeless area containing sparsely distributed sedges and grasses. Its mean daily maximum air temperatures are greater than 30°C every month, and the region experiences a short wet season from December to March and a long dry season from April to November. A substantial amount of rain falls during the wet season. Seventy five percent of the 1440 millimeters of mean annual rainfall falls during these few months. The increase in water levels within the Adelaide River floodplain is usually gradual. However, in March 2007, 244 mm of rain fell within 24 hours, causing a massive flood down the river. Since the flood coincided with a high tide, the floodwater was unable to exit into the sea, resulting in an "inland tsunami" with a wave height of 1 m. The wave reached the authors' study sites, and within a few hours, the entire river floodplain was completely underwater.

The study species were non-venomous water pythons (*Liasis fuscus*), which grow up to 3 meters in length. The snakes primarily feed on the dusky rat (*Rattus colletti*), a native rat species. Pythons often migrate for distances up to 10 kilometers during the wet season to track the movements of rat populations avoiding rising water levels. Data on water pythons was collected between 1991 and 2009, between the months of August and December on a 1.3 km long dam wall at Fogg Dam Conservation Reserve. The snakes were identified and captured at night with a spotlight, and were marked by clipping the ventral scale. The snout-vent length, mass, and female reproductive status were recorded for each python captured. Prey records were assessed through fecal and palpation analyses. The snakes were released 24 hours after being captured.

Dusky rat demographic data were collected during 5-day trapping periods every year in August. Since the floodplain at Fogg Dam was completely inundated, the researchers moved 5 km northeast to an area previously used for rice production (Rice Field). After assessing past data, the researchers found that rat numbers at Fogg Dam and Rice Field were highly correlated. Rice Field was also located within the pythons' wet season migratory region. Therefore, the authors resumed collecting rat demographic data at Rice Field.

The authors conducted additional snake trappings and rat demographic recordings at a second site, Beatrice Hill, after locating a large population of dusky rats inhabiting the area. The abundance of rats at Beatrice Hill contrasted to the virtual disappearance of rat populations observed at Rice Field. The rat population size at Rice Field plummeted after the large flood in 2007. Beatrice Hill was 8 km south of Rice Field and was situated near high ground.

Ujvari *et al.* analyzed the data with standard statistical analyses methods. To quantify the among-year variation in python body mass, the authors calculated residual body mass (RBM) from a general linear regression comparing python mass and snout-vent length. The survival rates and population numbers of the Fogg Dam water pythons were assessed using the Jolly-Seber model.

The authors found that the total numbers of rats captured at Rice Field varied among years, with rat populations dropping significantly after the "tsunami" in 2007. Only 7 rats were captured in 2007, none in 2008, and 4 in 2009. However, over 150 rats were captured at Beatrice Hill in 2009, which was higher than any rat numbers recorded during a trapping session throughout the 19-year study at Rice Field. A figure displaying the number of dusky rats captured at the Rice Field site from 1991 to 2009 and at Beatrice Hill in 2009 was constructed.

In accordance with the rat data collected at Rice Field and Beatrice Hill, Ujvari *et al.* captured a higher proportion of freshly fed snakes at Beatrice Hill (47 of 72) than at Rice Field (16 of 124). The pythons captured at Beatrice Hill had fed entirely on dusky rats. However, the pythons at Fogg Dam were emaciated and had a broader diet that included rats, snakes, and lizards.

The authors also found that python RBM varied among years and fluctuated with rat numbers. This suggests that the temporal variation in python RBM was driven by food (rat) availability. The mean RBM of pythons captured at Beatrice Hill in 2009 was significantly greater than the RBM of pythons captured at Fogg Dam throughout the researchers' 19-year study. In contrast, the RBM of pythons in 2008 and 2009 at Fogg Hill were the lowest RBM numbers ever recorded during the study. The low prey availability and low RBM for pythons at Fogg Dam during 2008 and 2009 reduced the annual python survival rate by 42%, which was significantly lower than the survival rate of pythons (79%) between 1987 and 2003. Ujvari *et al.* also did not capture any reproductive females at Fogg Dam during 2008 and 2009, resulting in no recruitment of yearling pythons in 2009. A figure displaying the RBM of water pythons from 1991 to 2009 was constructed. A graph demonstrating the linear relationship between number of rats and python RBM was also constructed.

Python population size was estimated to be 2183 $\pm$ 197 snakes in 2007, 1434 $\pm$ 175 snakes in 2008, and 536 $\pm$ 106 snakes in 2009. The population size in 2009 was the lowest number ever recorded during the study. Fogg Dam and Beatrice Hill also differed in their proportion of recaptured snakes. Of the 124 pythons captured at Fogg Dam in 2009, 33 were recaptures while all 72 pythons captured at Beatrice Hill were unmarked. This also indicates that the population size of Fogg Hill pythons was significantly lower than the population size of Beatrice Hill pythons.

These results demonstrate broad patterns of floodplain inundation, and rodent and snake responses to that inundation throughout the long-term study. The authors found that wet season rainfall increased the river's water levels, causing flooding throughout the Adelaide River floodplain. Therefore, only the levee banks along the river channel remained above the water. Rats congregated on these high points to avoid drowning, and in response, the pythons migrated to the levee banks to feed on the rodents. However, the "tsunami" in 2007 submerged the entire floodplain, including the levee banks. Although the authors cannot prove the flood was a result of climate change, it nevertheless acted as an extreme weather event that could increase in frequency with global warming. The authors' data suggest that this flood drowned the majority of the rats at Rice Field. Rats inhabiting regions along the floodplain edges survived by moving up to high ground, such as the high ground next to Beatrice Hill.

Ujvari *et al.* claimed that the spatial divergence in rat abundance caused the observed differences in python feeding rates and RBMs between the two sites. Therefore, feeding conditions for water pythons were better at Beatrice Hill than at Fogg Dam after the tsunami decimated the rat population at Rice Field. As a result, the Fogg Dam pythons ate less often and consumed other prey like smaller snakes and lizards, which caused their emaciation. The authors were unable to find a direct relationship between the reduction in python numbers at Fogg Dam and starvation rates. Yet, the lack of snake recruitment, lack of rats, the highly emaciated pythons, the strong relationship between python RBM and survival, and the increased snake mortality rates between 2008 and 2009 suggest that increased mortality caused the decrease in python population numbers in 2009. However, despite the lack of rats in the area, the pythons remained at Fogg Dam instead of searching out more the more abundant rat population at Beatrice Hill.

Ujvari *et al.* found that water pythons experienced a strong dry season philopatry. The pythons migrated great distances during the wet season in search of rats that moved to higher land to avoid flooding. Yet, the snakes always returned to their original territory when the dry season began since the water levels would usually subside, allowing large numbers of rats to return to the area. So, instead of searching out rat populations in different regions, the snakes returned to Fogg Hill because the beginning of the dry season had previously signaled the return of rats to their territory.

Overall, many predatory animals migrate to new locations by tracking prey abundance, and should therefore experience few difficulties moving to their prey's new ranges. However, other species, such as the water python, track the movement of their prey through habitat features that signal prey availability. Thus, if changes in climate alter these habitat attributes, predatory species may be unable to shift their activities to new areas. Therefore, climate change may pose a greater threat for mobile species than previously asserted.

Will Climate Change Reduce the Efficacy of Protected Areas for Amphibian Conservation in Italy?

Worldwide amphibian declines have been attributed to various interacting factors that include habitat loss and degradation, UV radiation, disease, and climate change. Recently, amphibian population disappearances within Italy have been associated with increasing temperatures, placing these species at great risk to climate change induced-extinction. Therefore, *in situ* conservation efforts such as integrating potential climate change impacts with the selection of protected areas within Italy are imperative to protecting amphibians. D'Amen *et al.* (2011) used a niche modeling estimate of potential amphibian range shift under two IPCC climate change scenarios and two dispersal assumptions to analyze amphibian extinction risk within Italy and to analyze the efficacy of the current Italian reserve network for protecting amphibian diversity. These predicted distributions were additionally used to perform gap and irreplaceability analyses to identify unprotected areas that could contribute to amphibian species conservation in the future. The results indicate that range alterations should be expected for all amphibian species under future climatic scenarios and that these range modifications will determine the degree to which species are represented within the Italian protected area network. Additionally, the results show that the existing protected area network incompletely represents total amphibian diversity and its geographic pattern, which ultimately will cause a decrease in species representation over the entire protected area system with climate change. Inclusion of the authors' suggested irreplaceable regions within the country could improve the future efficiency of the Italian protected area system.

The authors collected amphibian presence data from the CKmap 5.3.8 database, which reports species occurrence within the Universal Transverse Mercator (UTM, 10 X 10) grid that intersects the Italian region. Newly recognized amphibian species' distribution information was updated using maps from the IUCN Red List. To avoid small sample bias, species were excluded from the study if there were fewer than 20 records for these amphibian species. Alien species, cave species, and species only marginally present in Italy were also excluded. In total, the authors analyzed 22 species, 20 of which were ranked by the European Red List of Amphibians in the Low Concern Category.

D'Amen *et al.* calibrated niche-based models using climatic, land use, and topographical predictors. Of 20 predictor variables, only those that were correlated with a value of 0.70 or lower were used. The seven bioclimatic predictors used were annual mean temperature, mean diurnal temperature range, isothermality, temperature annual range, mean temperature of wettest quarter, precipitation of warmest quarter, and precipitation of coldest quarter. Their values were derived from the WorldClim database, which are climate grids for 1950–2000. Potential future climate values during 2041–2070 were obtained from climate grids of a previous study for IPCC scenarios A1F1 and B1 and from the HadCM3 circulation model. This model is commonly used for predicting climate change effects on fauna distribution in Europe. The authors selected A1F1 and B1 climate scenarios because they are based on contrasting story lines that cover a range of possible demographic, socio-economic and technological changes that are believed to affect green-house-gas emissions. The future climate scenarios were expressed as anomalies of past climate scenarios, interpolated, and then recombined with the grids from the WorldClim data set to produce high-resolution climate scenarios. The effects of existing land use on habitat availability, as well as topographic information, was included in the models.

Information on the location of existing protected areas in Italy was obtained from the National Ministry for the Environment. Protected areas within Italy consisted of Nationally Designed Protected areas (NPAs) and sites included in the European Natura 2000 network. The NPAs were composed of 774 parks founded by national or local administrations before 2004. They covered a surface area of 29,400 km². The Natura 2000 network was composed of 2885 sites that largely overlap with NPAs. Combined, they increased the protected area in Italy by 34,700 km². Natura 2000 areas that didn't overlap with NPAs were defined as EPAs. The Overall Protected Areas (OPAs) covered a total surface area of 64,100 km².

The authors experienced problems matching reserve boundaries with species distribution. Therefore, they used a threshold to determine whether reserves were considered present or absent in a grid cell. Numerous threshold values were tested (from 0% to 100%) and the value that resulted in the selection of a number of cells with a total surface equal to the total surface of Italian protected areas was used. Ultimately, the threshold was defined as any cell with a proportion of park coverage larger than 40%.

Amphibian species distributions were modeled using 8 different techniques within the R-based BIOMOD package. These models included Generalized Linear Models, Generalized Additive Models, Classification Tree Algorithms, Artificial Neural Networks, Mixture Discriminant Analysis, Multivariate Adaptive Regression Splines, Generalized Boosted Regression models, and Random Forest. The models were evaluated for their species distribution performance and consensus and those with the highest validation scores were included in the study. Since individual dispersal capability could restrict the ability of a species to geographically track suitable climatic conditions, species-specific dispersal limitations were considered. Additionally, the authors included a no-dispersal scenario since species range shifts are limited by extrinsic factors such as a highly fragmented landscape. These dispersal scenarios were used to estimate the proportion of current amphibian habitat that remained suitable under future climate conditions. Potential distributional shifts were calculated as the difference in the total number of grid cells currently occupied and those occupied under each of the future climate change scenarios.

Conservation targets for species conservation were used in both the gap and irreplaceability analyses. They were calculated by examining the species-specific extent of occurrence. These targets were later adjusted based on the modifications of the species range sizes under the future climatic scenarios. 1000 km^2 (10 cells) was defined as the minimum area needed for a species' viability. If species occupied area less than 10 cells, the conservation target was set to 100%. The conservation target of widespread species (those that occupied more than 1000 cells) was set at 10%. Conservation targets for species with intermediate sized ranges were determined by interpolating the extreme range size targets within a linear regression on the log transformed number of initially occupied cells.

A gap analysis was used to determine the extent of a species representation within the Italian reserve network by comparing amphibian species' distributions to the distributions of conservation areas. Species that were not represented in any protected area were defined as gap species and species that met a portion of their conservation target were considered to be partial gap species.

An irreplaceability analysis was used to measure the degree to which a cell was required in a reserve network to obtain the species-specific defined conservation targets. Irreplaceability was calculated as the number of combinations of sites that included the focal site and met conservation targets, but when the focal site was removed, the conservation targets would not be met. Current species occurrences and their future potential distributions under the different climate and dispersal scenarios were used to predict the irreplaceability of each cell. Three alternative conservation systems were considered (no reserves, NPAs, and OPAs) to assess the contribution of the existing reserve network.

Finally, the authors analyzed the efficacy of the existing Italian national park system (OPAs) and its components (NPAs and EPAs). They compared the mean irreplaceability value of cells in conservation networks to the mean value expected in cells randomly chosen regardless of their conservation status. The authors also tested whether OPAs and NPAs have higher irreplaceability than the remaining map cells, excluding the protected areas. The irreplaceability values of the new Natural 2000 sites were also calculated and incorporated into the analysis. Irreplaceability values were additionally recalculated considering the existence of NPAs for testing EPAs selection for current and future conservation.

A table displaying the current range extent and percentage of predicted change in the future climatic conditions under different dispersal assumptions was constructed, as was a second table displaying the percentages of target met by each species in NPAs and OPAs under present conditions and alternative dispersal and climate change scenarios. A figure showing the number of gap and partially gap species in the current conditions and in the future scenarios considering only NPAs and OPAs was constructed, as was a figure demonstrating the future irreplaceability patterns within Italy. Finally, a third table presenting the results of the non-randomness test of differences between the mean irreplaceability values in protected cells and in random cell selections was constructed.

The authors found that under a no-dispersal assumption, all but two species were projected to lose suitable habitat in the future climate scenarios. Although there was no statistically significant result, species range losses were generally higher under the A1F1 scenario. With dispersal ability, the models demonstrated that 50% of the species' range sizes would reduce by 60% under both climate scenarios. Eight species experienced a range reduction regardless of the climate change and dispersal scenarios. One species lost all suitable habitat under the A1F1 and no dispersal scenarios while four species experienced an increase in range size under the dispersal assumption.

Using the 40% threshold value, NPAs and OPAs occupied 282 cells and 617 cells total. All species were present in both the NPAs and OPAs. Nine species' conservation targets were met in the OPAs, but none were met when the analysis was restricted to NPAs. More than half of the partial gap species met less than 50% of their conservation targets and the predicted number of species that met conservation targets decreased in the future, irrespective of dispersal or climate change scenario. With NPAs, some species were predicted to become gap species and therefore disappear entirely from the currently protected cells. With OPAs, the number of species that met their conservation targets was projected to decrease. One species is projected disappear completely from the OPAs under the no-dispersal assumption.

Under the assumption of no protected cells, the areas with the highest values of irreplaceability for amphibian conservation were the island of Sardinia and the lowlands of Northeastern continental Italy. Secondary regions included Sicily and the Tyrrhenian side of Southern Italy. Included NPAs within the gap analysis reduced the irreplaceability scores for the grid cells within the Italian peninsula and on the Tyrrhenian side of Southern Italy.

Sardinia and Sicily had high irreplaceability values under both future climate scenarios and with no cells considered protected.

The cells on the Tyrrhenian side of Southern Italy, the cells in the mountainous areas of central and eastern Alps, and the cells in the central Apennine increased in irreplaceability as well. If all protected areas were considered present, the irreplaceability maps calculated for future conditions signified the focal areas that should be designated as new reserves for the long-term conservation of amphibians. These areas included Sardinia, the lowlands of Northeastern continental Italy, the central Alpine foothills, Sicily, and the Tyrrhenian side of Southern Italy.

Additionally, the comparison of mean irreplaceability values of protected map cells with values calculated from 5000 sets of randomly selected map cells demonstrate that the Italian network reserve (OPAs) and its components (NPAs and EPAs) protected sites with greater irreplaceability than that expected by chance. These results were constant under the future climate scenarios and under the no-dispersal assumption. With dispersal and under both climate scenarios, cells within NPAs were not more irreplaceable in the future than randomly selected cells, and cells within EPAs were only slightly more irreplaceable than the randomly chosen, unprotected cells. However, the reserve system as a whole had a larger irreplaceability value than the unprotected cells under future climatic scenarios.

The results show that the extent of species' range modifications under future climatic scenarios is dependent on dispersal ability. With dispersal, the models demonstrate that many species will be able to shift their ranges eastward and northward. Unfortunately, many amphibians may be unable to do so due to the highly fragmented landscape within Italy. Therefore, the no-dispersal assumption is the most realistic and under this assumption, and 70% of amphibians' predicted habitat is likely to be lost under future climatic scenarios.

The species most sensitive to climate chare are *P. fuscus, Salamandrina terdigitata, S. atra,* and *Triturus carnifex*. These species are either endemic or subendemic, but are classified as "Least Concern" in the most recent Red List of European Amphibians. Since a loss of distributional area is a good predictor of extinction risk, the results suggest that these species may become extinct within the middle of the current century. One subspecies in particular, *P. fuscus insubricus*, is endemic to the Po river plain of northern Italy and is recognized as a highly threatened taxon. By the mid 21st century, this subspecies may lose all suitable habitat under the assumption of no-dispersal. It is already difficult for this toad to navigate through its environmental matrix because of anthropogenic impact in the river plain. Therefore, the creation of corridors could allow this toad to disperse to areas with appropriate climate, assisting in its conservation.

Overall, the study indicates that all amphibian species will experience range modifications under the future climatic scenarios and that these modifications will determine the extent to which these species will be represented in the Italian protected area network. The current reserve network does not represent the entirety of amphibian diversity or its geographic pattern, decreasing the species' future representations within the reserve system. The reserve system would be improved as a whole if the study's suggested irreplaceable areas (Sicily, Sardinia, and Northeastern Italy) were included within the network.

Conclusions

Numerous endemic, specialist, and non-vagile species will be at risk from climate-induced extinction within the next 100 years if they are incapable of shifting their ranges along with their climate regimes. These species will be placed at further risk to extinction if other factors such as habitat fragmentation and land-use change combine with climatic variables to inhibit their persistence. Therefore, conservation efforts must not only consider protecting habitat areas where species' migrate to, but must also account for the areas in between species' old and new ranges that either facilitate or prevent their movements depending on their level of degradation. In some situations, natural migration may not be a viable option for species, especially immobile ones such as trees. Consequently, radical conservation efforts like translocation may have to be utilized. Through efforts such as these, earth's remaining, unique biodiversity may be preserved.

References Cited

Bohr, Y.E.M.B., Giertz, P., Ratovonamana, Y.R., Ganzhorn, J.U., 2011. Gray-Brown Mouse Lemurs (Microcebus griseorufus) as an Example of Distributional Constraints through Increasing Desertification. International Journal of Primatology 32:4, 901–913.

Chen, I., Hill, J.K., Ohlemuiler, R., Roy, D.B., Thomas, C.D., 2011. Rapid Range Shifts of Species Associated with High Levels of Climate Warming. Science 333, 1024–1026.

D'Amen, M., Bombi, P., Pearman, P.B., Schmatz, D.R., Zimmermann, N.E., Bologna, M.A., 2011. Will Climate Change Reduce the Efficacy of Protected Areas for Amphibian Conservation in Italy? Biological Conservation, 144: 989–997.

Dirnbock, T., Essl, F., Rabitsch, W., 2011. Disproportional risk for habitat loss of high-altitude endemic species under climate change. Global Change Biology, 990–996, doi: 10.1111/j.1365–2486.2010.02266.x

Erb, L.P., Ray, C., Guralnick, R., 2011. On the generality of a climate-mediated shift in the distribution of the American pika (Ochotona princeps). Ecology 92:9, 1730–1735.

Hargrove, L., and John T. Rotenberry, 2011. Breeding Success at the Range Margin of a Desert Species: Implications for a Cliamte-Induced Elevational Shift. Oikos 120: 1568–1576.

IPCC Fourth Assessment Report: Climate Change 2007. Climate Change 2007: Working Group I: The Physical Science Basis. How are Temperatures on Earth Changing? 2007.

http://www.ipcc.ch/publications_and_data/ar4/wg1/en/faq-3-1.html. Accessed 7 November 2011.

Mattila, N., Kaitala, V., Komonen, A., Paivinen, J. Kotiaho, J.S., 2011. Ecological Correlates of Distribution Change and Range Shift in Butterflies. Insect Conservation and Diversity. DOI: 10.1111/j.1752-4598.2011.00141.x

National Geographic Society. 2007. Mass Extinctions. What Causes Animal Die-Offs?. http://science.nationalgeographic.com/science/prehistoric-world/mass-extinction/. Accessed 7 November 2011.

Sandel, B., and Dangremond, E.M., 2011. Climate change and the invasion of California by grasses. Global Change Biology, doi: 10.1111/j.1365-2486.2011.02480.x

Ujvari, B., Shine, R., Madsen, T., 2011. How well do predators adjust to climate-mediated shifts in prey distribution? A study on Australian water pythons. Ecology 92: 3, 777–783.

2. Effects of Increased CO_2 on Agricultural Productivity

Taylor Jones

Atmospheric CO_2 is continually increasing and it is important to understand the potential effects of this trend on agricultural ecosystems and plant species worldwide. The potential of increasing CO_2 raises several critical questions: How will changes in CO_2 affect the global food supply? How will it affect plant biota? Are there any adaptations that could be advantageous to implement in order to enhance or curtail the effects of increasing CO_2? How does CO_2 interact with other factors of climate change such as drought, temperature, and various greenhouse gases? Increases in atmospheric CO_2 will inevitably occur simultaneously with other environmental factors of climate change and multi-factor interactions between CO_2 and other climate variables will ultimately determine how agricultural ecosystems respond. The balance of this chapter will investigate current scientific studies from 2011 that examine the effects of increasing CO_2 combined with other significant variables of climate change on agricultural productivity.

The study of the effects of increasing CO_2 emerged in the 1980s as researchers considered how plants would respond to the changes of a high-CO_2 world in short-run and long-run scenarios (Cure *et al.* 1986). Plants subject to increased CO_2 environments typically exhibit enhanced photosynthetic capabilities, with C_3 plants often being more responsive than C_4 plants (Rosenberg 1981). Several studies support the conclusion that under elevated CO_2, assuming an unchanged climate, plants will experience enhanced growth and increased water-use efficiency (Rosenberg 1982). Despite these potential gains, the important question remains: will plants continue to experience enhanced growth under enhanced CO_2 when other factors of climate change are involved? A more recent study conducted by Leakey and colleagues recognized that increasing temperature and altered soil composition due to climate change will likely reduce crop yields, but these detrimental factors might be offset by increases in atmospheric CO_2 (2006). They examined this condition by testing maize under ambient and elevated CO_2, measuring the photosynthesis, productivity and yield of the plant (Leakey *et al.* 2006). The study revealed that in the single location examined in North America, increased CO_2 in a drought-free environment did not significantly increase the photosynthesis or growth of maize and that increasing CO_2 conditions might not provide the full dividend expected in maize production (Leakey *et al.* 2006). Studies have also been conducted examining how more complex factors such as temperature, soil moisture and ozone levels interact with increasing CO_2 (Fuhrer 2003). Changes in agricultural productivity can occur at the plant level or at the agroecosystem level by inducing changes in nutrient cycling, predators, and crop-weed interactions (Fuhrer 2003). Contemporary studies of CO_2 enrichment build on previous studies similar to these and attempt to analyze the effects of increasing CO_2 in a multi-factor world affected by climate change.

This chapter will cover three main contemporary topics related to the effect of increased CO_2 on agriculture followed by a review paper that attempts to combine the findings of several previous studies. The first examines the effects of increased CO_2 on C_3 and C_4 plants subjected to different combinations of desiccation, temperature changes and varying CO_2 concentrations. Increased CO_2 also has significant effects on soil emissions of greenhouse gases, below ground nutrients, carbon sink, and overall yield, which represents the second topic. The third topic relates CO_2 enrichment studies to modern agricultural practices as it examines the relationship between toxin quantity and increased biomass in Bt transgenic crops in elevated CO_2 conditions. The final paper attempts to assemble a review of previous CO_2 enrichment studies and ultimately determine what can be learned from all of these studies. All of the following papers represent the most recent trends on CO_2 enrichment and represent detailed extensions of previous studies on the subject.

Increased Atmospheric CO_2 Levels and Warmer Weather Prevent Desiccation in C_4 Grassland

Grasslands and dry rangelands cover over 30% of the Earth's terrestrial surface and increased population growth is limiting the natural soil water supply in these areas. Changes in soil water supply depend on precipitation, temperature, CO_2 concentration, and various soil properties. Most of the world's livestock depend on this supply of grasslands to eat and survive, and climate change, including increased temperatures and CO_2 concentrations, may affect grass productivity. As CO_2 concentration increases, stomatal closure also increases allowing plants to retain more water and increase water-use efficiency. However, this increased efficiency may be due to increase overall biomass of the canopy level that results from an increase in CO_2. Most grasslands contain both C_3 and C_4 photosynthetic categories of plants and in the Prairie Heating and CO_2 Enrichment (PHACE) experiment reported here, Morgan *et al.* (2011) examined changes in plant productivity and soil water content in response to increases in CO_2. They concluded that increased CO_2 concentrations offset deleterious effects of increased temperature, maintaining soil water content at levels that occur today and increasing productivity in C_4 plants.

Jack A. Morgan and colleagues created the PHACE experiment to evaluate the responses of native mixed-grass prairie to one

year of increased CO_2 exposure and to a three year period of combined CO_2 exposure and increased temperatures. In 2006, the ambient CO_2 concentration was measured at the ambient level of 385
ppmv. It was experimentally increased to 600 ppmv. From 2007—
2009, the temperature was increased by 1.3/3.0° C (day/night) in the
canopy. The free-air CO_2 enrichment (FACE) was used to alter air
composition and the T-FACE system was used to alter the temperature. The authors found that increased temperature and increased
CO_2 concentration had opposite effects on soil water content (SWC).
As CO_2 increased, SWC also increased by 17.3%, as predicted by the
increased water efficiency due to more closed stomata. However, as
the temperature increased, SWC decreased by 13.1%. There was no
difference between the control (15.5%) and the combined increased
temperature and increased CO_2 plot, suggesting that the water conservation effects of increased CO_2 cancel out the drying effects of
warmer temperatures.

Using the same experimental design, the authors investigated
the effects of increased CO_2 concentration and increased temperature
on above-ground biomass (AGB) and below-ground biomass (BGB),
both estimates of a plant's productivity and growth. As expected, the
prairie exposed to increased levels of CO_2 increased the amount of
above-ground biomass by an average 33% over the first three years,
supporting the benefits of CO_2 enrichment on plant productivity and
growth. The same positive effect of increased CO_2 concentration ap-
peared for the growth in roots composing the BGB. To continue the
study of the effects of increased CO_2 on SWC and plant productivity,
Morgan *et al.* examined how these changes in AGB related to the soil
matric potential (energy of soil water per unit volume) using the biomass enhancement ratio. A strong negative correlation between the
soil matric potential and the biomass enhancement ratio resulted and
is likely due to the increased water efficiency under conditions of high
CO_2 concentrations and shows that increased CO_2 concentration will
increase productivity when water is limited. Morgan *et al.* also com-

pared the results of this portion of the experiment with results from other similar areas of the Great Plains.

Through these experiments, the authors distinguished significant differences between C_3 and C_4 grasses. C_3 grasses showed 34% more growth during increased CO_2 conditions, but increases in temperature did not have an effect. C_4 grasses showed 28% more growth during increased CO_2 conditions but also increased growth during warming, suggesting that C_4 grasses could be more productive in future atmospheric conditions of high CO_2 and increased temperature. The results also suggest that increased CO_2 concentration may counter the effects of extreme dryness due to increased temperatures in the future. The authors also created a model analysis that changed the canopy resistance to water loss (change in stomatal closure) through various temperatures and recorded the effects on the evapotranspiration rate (the combined rate of evaporation and transpiration of the prairie). The results showed that the temperature effect and the increased CO_2 effect almost exactly offset one another. Despite this trend, the authors predict the efficiency advantages of increased CO_2 will not be able to offset extreme drought conditions and regions like southwestern North America or the Mediterranean may not benefit from these effects. The results from this experiment only show one example of the benefits of increased CO_2 in a semi-arid plant community, but it is clear that under certain circumstances, increased CO_2 concentration can increase plant efficiency and water use.

The Combined Effects of Increasing Temperature and CO_2 on the Growth of C_3 and C_4 Annual Species

With CO_2 levels predicted to rise in the future, several recent experiments have investigated the effects of increasing CO_2 on plant growth and development. Studies on cool weather C_3 annual plants have demonstrated enhanced photosynthesis under elevated CO_2 when other environmental factors remain constant. The ability to increase growth under elevated CO_2 could be very beneficial for C_3 crops, enhancing productivity and increasing yield. Warm weather C_4 annual plants have generally been less responsive to increases in atmospheric CO_2 levels, demonstrating similar levels for photosynthesis at various levels of CO_2. However, studies have shown that increases in both temperature and CO_2, a more realistic scenario, demonstrate an ecological advantage for C_4 plants as the advantages of C_3 plants decline with an increase in temperature. Rising CO_2 is also expected to significantly affect the reproductive structures of both C_3 and C_4 plants, due to high temperature shocks during fertilization, inhibiting vital growth stages. Despite increasing literature on the effects of climate change on plants, few studies have examined the impacts of increased temperature and elevated CO_2 on weedy plants or grasses. In this study, Lee examined the effects of increased temperature, and increased temperature with elevated CO_2 on two annual species of C_3 and C_4 plants, *Chenopodium album* and *Setaria viridis* respectively. The author found that elevated temperature significantly affects the biomass production in the reproductive stages and this effect may be enhanced for C_3 plants. However, the disadvantages of warming are countered in the presence of elevated CO_2 in C_3 plants.

Lee assembled three experimental plots subjected to varying condition, the first being a control with ambient CO_2 and temperature. The second plot (T4) was subjected to a 4°C increase in temperature with ambient CO_2 and the third plot (CT4) was subjected to a 4°C increase in temperature along with 1.8 times the ambient CO_2 level. The plots were rotated to minimize the effects of inadvertent variations in light, air temperature, and CO_2 concentration. The biomass of the plants was estimated using the plant size index and was measured at two week intervals throughout the growing period. Leaf area and photosynthesis rates were also recorded. Emerging seedlings and flower number were counted after at least one seedling shoot extended 0.2 cm.

Throughout this study, Lee found that seedling emergence and flowering times in C_3 and C_4 plants were significantly advanced under T4 and CT4 conditions compared to the control, however the differences between these two conditions was relatively small. The date of emergence of *C. album* seedlings was 27.0 and 24.3 days early in T4 and CT4 plots respectively, compared to the control. Also, the length of the flowering time increased significantly in T4 and CT4 scenarios compared to the control in *S. viridis*, but not in the C_3 plant. Lee concluded that since most of the differences were between the control and T4 or CT4 plots, plant phenology is likely affected more by the increase of temperature than the elevation of CO_2. Also, the seedling emergence time of *S. viridis* was more sensitive to increased temperature than that of *C. album* which could lead to serious implications for population establishment when seeds are competing for resources and space. The author concludes that C_4 plants will have an advantage in this scenario due to the increased sensitivity to temperature.

Throughout the growth stages, the mean temperatures in the plots subjected to elevated temperature remained approximately equal, indicating that the temperatures during critical growth stages were about the same for C_3 and C_4 plants. The changes in temperature were accounted for by advancing plant phenology. However, these conditions of ideal light and temperature are not realistic and changing plant phenology also affects the solar radiation intensity. Lee determined that accumulated solar radiation decreased by 19% and 16.1% in C_3 and C_4 plants respectively in T4 conditions and this decrease in solar radiation led to decreases in biomass production. It is likely that these decreases in biomass production would be compensated for in an increased temperature and CO_2 environment.

The effect of elevated CO_2 seemed to be greater when coupled with increases in temperature, which led to a significant increase in photosynthesis in C_3 plants. In this study, elevated CO_2 levels and temperature increased the rate of photosynthesis in C_3 plants and increased biomass production when compared to ambient conditions. Increased temperature did not significantly affect the biomass production of C_4 plants, maintaining their advantage in T4 and CT4 conditions as a result of resistance to increasing temperature and CO_2. Based on this study, C_3 plants are predicted to have an advantage under future global warming conditions as they can avoid the detrimental effects of high temperatures during the vegetative growth stage by flourishing under increased CO_2.

Interspecific Effects of Elevated CO_2 on Seed Production in C_3 Plants

Atmospheric CO_2 was estimated to be 280µmol mol^{-1} before the industrial revolution era and is currently estimated at 390µmol mol^{-1} with predictions to increase in the future. Several vital plant functions, such as photosynthesis, transpiration, and biomass are affected by increases in atmospheric CO_2 levels. For wild plants, seed quantity and quality influence their fitness and seed production, and in the presence of elevated CO_2, this varies considerably among species of C_3 annual plants. In this study, Hikosaka *et al.* perform a meta-analysis to examine whether seed production is limited by nitrogen availability or concentration. In general, studies have shown that increased ambient CO_2 leads to increased N per plant and increased seed production, as seed mass per plant has increased by 28–35%. However, this study shows that various species respond differently, and understanding these differences is important to maintaining C_3 plant productivity in an enriched CO_2 world. The authors predict that the N contained in reproductive organs accounts for the variation in the increased CO_2 response of seed production.

Kouki Hikosaka and colleagues performed a meta-analysis to examine the variation of seed production in annual C_3 plants under increased CO_2 concentrations. The enhancement ratio of seed mass per plant due to increased CO_2 was 0.75–4.45 for rice, 0.93–1.87 for soybean, and 0.88–2.07 for wheat, but these differences could be attributed to different growth conditions. The authors also determined that seed production is not linked to change in total plant biomass. For example, a study cited by Jablonski *et al.* reported increases in fruit and seed yield of 12% and 25% respectively with a 31% increase in total plant mass. CO_2 responses also differ between reproductive tissues in different species. The boll yield of cotton increased by 40% and lint increased by 54%. Studies also demonstrate an increase in pod wall mass of soybeans and greater increases in mass of reproductive structures of *Xanthium canadense* in low N environments compared to high N environments.

Hikosaka and colleagues also examined N use in reproductive growth and CO_2 response and hypothesized that the differences in response to increased CO_2 are either a result of different limiting factors (such as CO_2 or N) or a constant N limitation. Compilations of studies showed that the seed mass of C_3 plants grown at varying levels of CO_2 was not correlated with N concentration, but rather demonstrated a 1:1 correlation between seed mass per plant and N per plant. This supports the second hypothesis that seed production is only enhanced when N is more readily available.

Seed N levels experienced variation in some species more than others and may be enhanced in some plants by absorbing more during growth or retranslocating N from vegetative to reproductive organs. The N-fixing legumes showed the greatest N enhancement, but significant variation in other areas such as biomass, photosynthetic rates, and leaf-area index. In several studies, the N concentration in seeds remained the same while vegetative N concentrations decreased, showing that the vegetative organs are less conservative. The authors also examined seed N per plant and seed N concentration of three species: grass, legumes, and non-legume dicots. The studies showed increases in seed mass per plant in the presence of elevated CO_2 and increases in seed N per plant for legume species.

Three quarters of variation in seed-mass enhancement was attributed to increases in seed N per plant, while one quarter was attributed to reductions in N concentration. The reduction of N concentration was noticed most in legumes, and not as much in the other species. Also, in several grass species, the presence of albumen allowed storage of high amounts of carbohydrates while N levels were low.

Overall, N limitation is key to understanding seed production and responses in elevated CO_2 environments. Plants experience increased seed production when they undergo increased N acquisition or decreased N concentration. Legumes are N-fixing and grasses often experience increases in seed production through increases in N acquisition and decreases in N concentration. Decreases in N concentration may not decrease the quality of the seeds if it results from increased albumen content without reduced N in embryos.

Increased Soil Emissions of Potent Greenhouse Gases under Increased Atmospheric CO_2

Burning fossil fuels and frequently changing land use contribute to rapidly increasing atmospheric CO_2 levels. An increase in CO_2 can alter both abiotic and biotic conditions of soil and affect the levels of other important greenhouse gases (GHG) such as nitrous oxide (N_2O) and methane (CH_4). Several previous studies have shown that increased CO_2 levels could slow climate change by increasing plant efficiency and soil carbon input and storage, however CO_2 should not be examined alone because other gases also have high global warming potentials. For example, N_2O and CH_4 have global warming potentials 298 times higher and 25 times higher respectively than that of CO_2. In this study, Van Groenigen *et al.* (2011) examined the effects of increased atmospheric CO_2 on N_2O levels in upland soil and CH_4 levels in rice paddies and natural wetlands and concluded that changes in these greenhouse gases can greatly affect how ecosystems influence climate change.

Kees Jan van Groenigen and colleagues completed a meta-analysis on 152 observations from 49 published studies to examine fluxes of CH_4 and N_2O in the presence of increased CO_2. GHG emissions span a variety of ecosystems and the compiled meta-analysis, compared to an individual experiment, provides a more comprehensive study. The increased CO_2 stimulated N_2O emissions in uplands by 18.8% and stimulated CH_4 in wetlands by 13.2% and in rice paddies by 43.4%. The authors also examined the effect of increased CO_2 on the possible causes for these changes in GHG emissions, soil water content and root biomass. Combining all three types of terrain, soil water content increased 6% and root biomass increased 18%.

The authors also investigated the importance of the changes in GHG levels on fertilized (agricultural) and non-fertilized (natural) land. The model was tested on current CO_2 levels to confirm the accuracy of the scaling approach. NO_2 stimulation in agricultural uplands indicated an increased 0.33 Pg CO_2 equivalents per year and an increased 0.24 Pg CO_2 equivalents per year in natural areas. CH_4 stimulation in agricultural rice paddies indicated an increased 0.25 Pg CO_2 equivalents per year and an increased 0.31 Pg CO_2 equivalents per year in natural wetlands. In addition, carbon sink was larger for fertilized areas and GHG emissions could cancel the expected increase in carbon sink by 16.6%, based on the authors' calculations.

Van Groenigen and colleagues present three reasons that suggest this increase of carbon sink could be an underestimate because first, the majority of data collected during the growing season and some terrains have higher N_2O emissions during the winter that could add up to 7% more N_2O. Second, N_2O emissions increased in studies that included additional nitrogen, so as nitrogen increases along with CO_2, N_2O levels may also increases. Last, the authors noticed a weak correlation between experiment duration and so the effect of CO_2 is likely to increase over time.

Increased CO_2 levels stimulate denitrification, a major contributor to N_2O levels in upland soil and in wetlands and rice paddies of various geographic regions, methanogenic archaea rely heavily on carbon levels as a source of organic substrates and with increased CO_2

levels, more CH_4 is produced. This study shows that not only do increased CO_2 levels amplify climate change, but the increase of N_2O in uplands and CH_4 in wetlands and rice paddies could negate carbon sink percentages and further studies should consider the indirect effects of these other greenhouse gases on climate change.

Elevated CO_2 Leads to Long-Term Forest Productivity and Increases in Carbon Flux

With rising levels of atmospheric CO_2 due to climate change, the earth is becoming more dependent on changes in ambient air composition and its effect on plant growth and productivity. Recent studies have shown significant variety in ecosystem responses to enriched CO_2 environments and only some studies demonstrated increased rates of NPP. In the following experiment, Drake *et al.* (2011) examine the physiological responses of loblolly pine (*Pinus tadea*) trees to increased CO_2 and determine the effects on nutrient availability and uptake. The experiment was performed on the grounds of Duke's FACE program and the authors collected data on a variety of physiological plant factors in ambient and enriched CO_2 to determine if the information from this testing site can be applied to other ecosystems. It was predicted that increases in carbon flux, nitrogen-uptake and overall plant productivity would lead to long-term forest enrichment.

John E. Drake and colleagues started the experiment with 3-year-old loblolly trees planted 2.4 by 2.4 meters apart. In 1994, they began collecting data on the paired reference plots and in 1996, began collecting data in all additional plots. Some data was taken from previous research at the FACE testing site and some data was new for this experiment. The standing pool of fine root biomass was measured every three months by collecting a 4.65 cm block of soil 15 cm deep and analyzing it for C content. The amount of C stored as CO_2

in the soil air space was calculated and the microbial biomass of N was measured.

The rate of CO_2 diffusion out of the soil (soil CO_2 efflux) was measured with the closed IKGA system and the data were plotted as a temperature response curve. The fine root production was measured monthly and the production of various fungi was measured using microscopic methods. The on-site litterfall was collected monthly January–September and biweekly October–December in 12 baskets per site, measuring $0.218m^2$ each. The authors also collected data on C-cycling, NPP and total belowground carbon flux (TBCF).

The results showed that as CO_2 increased, the rate of C-cycling through the soil increased by 17%. Also, the TBCF increased 16% and the increased C entering the soil in an enriched CO_2 environment led to increases in the net biomass. N also increased, supporting an increase in NPP, supplied by a 25% increase in soil uptake. TBCF and N-uptake demonstrated an inverse relationship. NPP positively correlated with canopy N content and supported an increase in photosynthetic N-use efficiency.

Drake *et al.* suggest that the increase in productivity is due to an exchange of tree C with soil N belowground, allowing the N levels to meet the growth requirements of the plant. Also, the long-term NPP increases are likely enabled by increases in TBCF that stimulate N-uptake and canopy leaf area. Despite increased productivity, the experiment did not result in a net accumulation of C in the mineral soil pool. The authors suggest this could be a result of the fixed C being added to the experiment replacing some of the C initially present in the soil and increases in microbial activity could account for changes in the soil composition. This effect on C pools is likely to model the response of soil to a long-term rise in CO_2. The authors recognize that this study provides an initial attempt to examine the physiological effects of increases CO_2, but is by no means comprehensive and further experiments representing a diversity of effects are necessary to better understand the long-term effects of increased CO_2.

A simple experimental framework describing the most important processes that effect N availability and C uptake is necessary to understand the effects of CO_2 enrichment in the future.

Negative Effects of Increased Temperature and O_3 Offset Positive Effects of CO_2 in Oilseed Rape (*Brassica napus* L.)

CO_2 in the atmosphere is steadily increasing and is predicted to be 500–1000 ppm by the end of the century. Emissions of other greenhouse gases are also increasing and are expected to raise the surface temperature 1.8–4.0° C, along with increasing emissions of ozone (O_3) from human activity. These forces, and many others, naturally act together and have an important effect on agricultural productivity and climate change. It is more useful and practical to study the effects of multiple, layered factors of climate change than to study one factor in isolation. For example, increased CO_2 alone will increase the photosynthetic rate in plants, increasing biomass production, and result in positive growth for plants. However, this increase in biomass does not necessarily lead to an increase in crop yield. It is important to combine and test the effects of various factors of climate change on crops to determine potential crop yield because with a growing human population, maximizing crop yield is highly desirable. Plants do not have many natural adaptations for living in conditions with increased CO_2, so it is important to study how they react in order to better breed and genetically prepare plants for climate change.

Frenk and colleagues controlled the ambient conditions of four cultivars of oilseed rape (*Brassica napus* L.) of different ages and origins and exposed each cultivar to a different combination of increased CO_2 (700 ppm), increased temperature (+5°C), and increased O_3 (60 ppb). The plants were raised in growth chambers and at the end of maturation, ten plants from each cultivar were selected at random to study. The pod, stem height, and stem width were recorded along with seed yield, stem weight, and biomass. The Thousand Seed

Weight (TSW) and Harvest Index (HI) were determined for each sample.

Increased temperature alone generally reduced the seed yield by 38–58%, the total number of seeds, and the mass of seeds and pods. Despite these general trends, variability among cultivars only produced a significant difference in seed yield for two of them. Stem biomass was not significantly different with increased temperature, and only one cultivar showed a difference in stem weight. The low total seed yield also reduced the HI. The authors predict the decrease in biomass typically associated with increased temperatures is due to reduced rates of photosynthesis, quick development, increased respiration, and decreased organ development. Plant breeding today is often focused on yield, so these new plants will likely be the most susceptible to climate change and the negative effects of increased temperature.

Increased CO_2 alone resulted in a general increase in total seed yield (only significant for one plot) and the total number of seeds. Stem height increased for all cultivars and biomass increased in general, but was only significant for one cultivar. Frenk *et al.* predict that the effects of increased CO_2 can be offset over time because the plant does not have enough storage organs and has reduced carbon sink capacity.

Increased O_3 alone had no effect on plant yield or stem weight, but combined with temperature, O_3 further reduced the positive effects of increased CO_2, and further decreased yield. When CO_2 and temperature both increased, they equalized the effects of one another and the sample resembled the control in biomass growth and yield. According to Frenk and colleagues, no study to date has examined the combined effects of the three factors discussed above on agricultural productivity and the results show significant changes in agricultural productivity and should be combined with more abiotic and biotic factors in the future to determine the full effects of increased CO_2.

Estimated Magnitude of Persistent Carbon Sink in World's Forests

Forests are important in absorbing a significant amount of CO_2 in the earth's atmosphere. It is necessary to understand how much of an effect they have in order to set limitations on greenhouse gas emissions and better understand the effects of climate change. The Intergovernmental Panel on Climate Change (IPCC) reports a wide range of data on the C uptake by terrestrial ecosystems, stating that uptake could range from less than 1.0 to 2.6 Pg per year. More recent models on climate change report a C sink range of 2.0 to 3.4 Pg per year. Understanding and constraining these limitations is crucial in understanding the future effects of climate change. In this report, the authors carried out a bottom-up estimation of C stocks and changes based on recent data and long-term field observations coupled with statistical modeling. The C pools in forest include measurements from dead wood, harvested wood, living biomass, litter, and soil. Data from different countries, regions, and continents was compared to understand trends across geographic boundaries. The area examined contains 3.9 billion ha, which accounts for 95% of the world's forests.

Yude Pan and colleagues report the estimated amount of carbon stock in the world's forests at 861 ± 66 Pg C of which 44% resides in soil, 42% in live biomass, 8% in dead wood, and 5% in litter. Breaking down the C sink by types of forests, tropical forests account for 471 ± 93 Pg C, boreal forests 272 ± 23 Pg C, and temperate forests 119 ± 6 Pg C. Tropical and boreal forests store most of the earth's carbon, however tropical forests have 56% in above ground biomass and boreal forests only have 20% in above ground biomass. This difference is crucial in determining what precautions should be taken to preserve certain parts of forests in different regions. The annual change in C stock shows an uptake of 2.5 ± 0.4 Pg C per year for 1990 to 1999 and 2.3 ± 0.5 Pg C per year from 2000 to 2007.

Despite the overall C uptake in these two time periods, regional differences are apparent. For example, temperate forests increased C sink by 17% more from 2000 to 2007 compared to 1990 to 1999, while tropical forests decreased C sink by 23% during the same time period. By subtracting the C sink losses from forest degradation in tropical areas, the net forest C sink is estimated at 1.0 ± 0.8 and 1.2 Pg C per year from 1990 to 1999 and 2000 to 2007, respectively.

Examining C sink by region and biome, boreal forests had an estimated C sink of 0.5 ± 0.1 Pg C per year for the past two decades. Some regions, such as Asian Russia, account for a significant portion of the total sink, but experienced no overall change. Other areas, like European Russia, experienced a 35% increase in C sink. The authors suggest this increase could be due to increased forest area after agricultural abandonment, reduced harvesting or several areas of forest progressing to later stages in the plant life cycle. The C sink in Canadian forests reduced by half during the same time period, largely due to wildfires and insect outbreaks. As a result of the increases and decreases mentioned above, the overall C sink did not experience a net change.

Temperate forests contributed 0.7 ± 0.1 and 0.8 ± 0.1 Pg C per year for the past two decades. This increase in C sink is likely due to increases in density of forest biomass and an increase in forest area. The C sink in the U.S. on average increased by 33% during this time period due to the growth of forest area resulting from previous agriculture and harvesting. However, the western U.S. has experienced forest mortality due to drought stress, insects, and fires. The C sink in Europe remained constant, but the C sink in China increased by 34%, likely due to newly planted forest area and reforestation programs.

Tropical forests account for about 70% of the world's forests and in this study, the authors collected data from intensive monitoring of Africa and South America, and used these trends to estimate the data for Southeast Asia. The total C sink in tropical forests is estimated at 1.3 ± 0.3 and 1.0 ± 0.5 Pg C per year for the past two decades. The total C sink during this time period accounts for about half of the total C sink. Tropical land use, including clearing forests for agriculture, timber and pasture areas, accounts for a carbon release second to the amount produced by fossil fuels. Deforestation accounted for about 40% of global fossil fuel emissions in the past two decades, but this is often overlooked because it was offset by a large uptake in C due to forest regrowth. Pan and colleagues estimate that C uptake was stronger in regrowth forests compared to previously intact forests due to simultaneous rapid increases in biomass. The authors also suggest that the state tropical forests has a significant impact on total C sink and better monitoring techniques and increased understanding of C cycling in these areas should be a priority in the future.

Dead wood, litter, soil, and harvested wood account for about 35% of the world's forest C sink and are important factors that should not be overlooked, however they remain the most difficult to measure. This measurement could also be too low as it does not include deep soil beyond 1 meter and improved measuring techniques would be necessary to account for this. Dead wood is more vulnerable to fires than other sources of C and harvested wood in boreal areas experienced a decrease over the past two decades, mainly due to decreased Russian harvesting.

Pan and colleagues recognize critical data gaps in their study including a substantial lack of data for North America (mainly Canadian unmanaged forests and Alaska), and for the C flux in tropical forests, which may account for a 10–20% error in estimates. The authors suggest that in order to attempt to combat these uncertainties, land monitoring should be increased, globally consistent land-sensing is necessary, and scientists need better tools to measure below ground, dead wood and litter sources of C.

Forests have a crucial role in absorbing atmospheric C and will continue to maintain strong control over atmospheric CO_2 levels.

The factors that affect C levels in the atmosphere are complex and it is necessary to adopt better monitoring systems to separate their impacts and determine the effects of climate change. The authors note that although a large amount of CO_2 humans place in the atmosphere is sequestered by forests, deforestation significantly contributes to C losses and relying on forests to absorb C is not without risk.

The Effects of Increased CO_2 on Biomass and Exogenous Toxin Quantity in Transgenic Bt Cotton and Rice Crops

Transgenic crops have become an increasingly important component of modern agroecosystems, ideally providing environmentally friendly, disease resistant crops with combinations of multiple genes that improve productivity and agricultural yield. One of the most common types of transgenic crop is *Bacillus thuringiensis* ("Bt"), which is produced worldwide and exhibits a strong resistance to lepidopteran pests in multiple cropping environments. With CO_2 levels expected to increase in the future, scientists question the ability of Bt crops to adapt to changing atmospheric conditions and some hypothesize that increasing CO_2 will pose new ecological risks for Bt crops and possibly reduce their effectiveness against target pests. In this study, a series of open-top chamber (OTC) experiments were conducted to asses whether measured exogenous-toxin quantity is reduced in transgenic Bt cotton and rice due to increased plant biomass under elevated atmospheric CO_2. This study also examines the effectiveness of Bt cotton and rice transgenes against *H. armigera* and *C. suppressalis* larvae respectively. The study showed that there are significant differences between the exogenous-toxin levels of Bt cotton and rice under increased CO_2 and both showed differences in toxin quantity among developmental stages. Also, the new properties of Bt crops under elevated CO_2 significantly affected the performance of *H. armigera* and *C. suppressalis* larvae, despite the adverse effects of Bt gene expression in elevated CO_2 conditions.

Chen and colleagues performed a series of OTC experiments with ambient (375μl/L) and elevated (750μl/L) CO_2 conditions that were maintained via a continuous automatic control system. Thirty-six pots of transgenic Bt cotton and twenty-six pots of transgenic Bt rice were planted and their positions were randomized each day to limit positional effects in the OTC chambers. In select plots, cotton bollworm (*H. armigera*) and rice stem borer *C. suppressalis* were added to examine the effects of pest larvae on Bt cotton and rice. Biomass index was used to determine the increased amount of biomass under elevated CO_2 conditions and plant tissues were tested for exogenous-toxin quantity. Chen *et al.* recognize the potential "dilution effect" in which percent biomass increase exceeds the percent increase in exogenous-toxin increase, resulting in decreased levels of exogenous-toxin.

The results show that increasing CO_2 levels significantly increased leaf, petiole, shoot and total plant biomass production of 45-DAS ("days after seedling") Bt cotton as well as increases in shoot and total plant biomass production in 90-DAS cotton. Similar trends resulted for Bt rice as root, above-ground, and total stem biomass increased in 50-DAS rice and root tissues increased in 100-DAS rice. Overall, elevated levels of CO_2 led to increased biomass in Bt cotton and rice, as predicted by previous studies showing increased photosynthesis and growth rates.

Elevated CO_2 conditions significantly reduced exogenous-toxin content in both Bt cotton and rice tissues. However, the effect of CO_2 level on exogenous-toxin amount varied among crops and their respective plant tissues. For example, increased CO_2 significantly reduced exogenous-toxin content per plant in 45-DAS and 90-DAS Bt cotton, while simultaneously increasing exogenous-toxin content in the stems of 50-DAS Bt rice. This shows that the responses of transgenic Bt cotton and rice (relating to exogenous-toxin content) to increased ambient CO_2 are different. Also, each plant exhibited different responses in different phases of development. Chen and colleagues compared percent changes in biomass and exogenous-toxin levels and concluded that a dilution effect exists in shoot and petiole tissues of 45-DAS Bt cotton and in root, above-ground, and total stem tissues of 50-DAS Bt rice as well as leaf sheaths of 100-DAS rice. This is probably related to increased plant nitrogen-use efficiency and the authors predict that increased plant carbohydrate concentration diluted Bt proteins. For other increases in exogenous-toxin levels, the authors conclude that the dilution effect is only partly responsible and the reduction is due to reduced expression of the Bt gene under increased CO_2 conditions.

The results also suggest that most *H. armigera* larvae preferred to feed on transgenic Bt cotton squares and bolls, and most *C. suppressalis* larvae preferred to feed upon leaf sheaths of transgenic Bt rice. These areas of the Bt crops correlate with decreases in exogenous-toxin production, as expected. Although feeding increased in certain areas, the study found overall decreases in larval survival rate and pupal weight of *H. armigera* and *C. suppressalis*, suggesting that the Bt cotton and rice in this study to not face serious risks of reduced efficiency against pests in increased CO_2 conditions.

A Review of CO_2 Enrichment Studies: Does Enhanced Photosynthesis Enhance Growth?

Plants typically only convert 2 to 4% of available energy into actual growth and this natural inefficiency provides a reason for scientists to attempt to increase the efficiency of the process by increasing photosynthesis. One of the most common methods, other than genetic modification, to increase photosynthesis is to increase ambient CO_2. Elevated CO_2 can lead to growth increases ranging from 10 to 50%, depending on the plant's carbon sink capacity and nutrient availability. Previous studies show that elevated CO_2 inevitably leads to increased growth, but the magnitude of the growth varies with the photosynthetic capacity of the plant. Photosynthesis is an inefficient process with a maximum of 8 to 10% of the energy in sunlight being converted into chemical energy. Realistically, only 2 to 4% of energy in sunlight is converted. In this paper, Kirschbaum examines previous studies and conducts experiments of his own in order to summarize the current knowledge on CO_2 enrichment studies, focusing on the ability of increased photosynthesis to ultimately increase plant growth. Kirschbaum studies the factors that affect plant growth under elevated CO_2 in an attempt to determine if photosynthesis is the main factor increasing growth or if other factors are relatively more important.

Kirschbaum first examines the photosynthetic response to increasing CO_2 concentrations and distinguishes between Rubisco-limited photosynthetic rates and ribose 1,5-bisphosphate (RuBP) re-generation-limited rates. For both photosynthetic rates, the relative responsiveness of increases in CO_2 concentration decreases as atmos-pheric CO_2 continues to increase. Photosynthesis is limited by Rubisco-limited rates at low CO_2 concentrations and RuBP regenera-tion-limited rates at high concentrations, and scientists argue that the amounts of Rubisco plants have today is in excess of what is needed, so most plants experience RuBP regeneration-limited photosynthesis. Changes in plant photosynthesis are supported by previous studies, as 30 to 40% enhancements in photosynthesis were recently found in free-air CO_2 enrichment experiments and a 58% increase was found in a controlled plot experiment. Kirschbaum notes that there are im-portant limitations to any photosynthesis study as plants that experi-ence less light and increased self-shading may have less enhancement of photosynthesis, while plants grown in high temperature conditions may have more. On average, increases in ambient CO_2 lead to a 30% enhancement of photosynthesis, but does this translate to a 30% en-hancement of growth?

Studies show that the relative growth rate for plants is often similar among species and enhanced photosynthesis often leads to only a 10% increase in the relative growth rate. Kirschbaum suggests that previous studies show an increases in photosynthesis leads to 20% enhanced leaf area, but also a 6.5% increase in leaf weight due to increase amounts of carbohydrates and this leads to an ineffective transformation of increased photosynthetic rates to new growth. Extra amounts of carbon produced from photosynthesis can only be of use if the plant can utilize it through root growth, new foliage, or other carbon sinks. Also, carbon cannot be used efficiently if other vital resources, such as nitrogen, are lacking. Studies have shown that many plants show strong photosynthetic enhancement during the growth stages, reduced enhancement during the flowering stages and then increased enhancement during the fruiting stages. During the flowering stages, plants lost much of their potential carbon sink that exists in the growth phase and is regained through seed production in the flowering stage. Most plants show some increased growth response to elevated CO_2, but the degree of this growth is determined by other limiting factors, such as carbon sink and nitrogen availability.

Kirschbaum also notes that a large number of papers use biomass enhancement ratios to determine the effects of elevated CO_2 on plant growth. Biomass enhancement ratios are often much greater than relative growth rates and also greater for single-plant studies and fast-growing plants. Under elevated CO_2, plants often experience exponential growth in early stages, followed by average growth rates in intermediate stages. Plants that experience an overall relative growth rate of 10% can experience a biomass enhancement ratio of 50% in intermediate stages which eventually decreases to about 10% in later stages. This concept explains why fast-growing plants can have higher biomass enhancement ratios compared to slower-growing plants, but the same relative growth rate. Therefore, the length of an experiment is very important and should be considered when examining the biomass enhancement ratio of a plant to determine if real growth increases exist. The biomass enhancement ratio can often be a misleading value as it can be manipulated by varying the length of an experiment.

Kirschbaum identifies other issues that may affect photosynthetic enhancement rates that need to be considered, such as natural competition and growth response in mixed-species communities. Also, some studies have shown a decrease in protein concentrations under elevated CO_2. Plant herbivore interactions might also change as elevated CO_2 usually leads to lower nutrient concentrations which reduces the rate of herbivores feeding on the plant and as a result, herbivores may attempt to consume more of the plant. All of these factors are important complicating issues and should be addressed further.

In conclusion, photosynthetic enhancement due to elevated CO_2 increases the carbon available to plants and whether or not this translates to growth depends on other colimiting factors, such as nutrient availability and carbon sink. Increases in carbon will exacerbate any other limitations. Plants are also subjected to genetic constraints and will only respond to increases in photosynthesis to levels within their genetic capability. By examining several CO_2 enrichment experiments, Kirschbaum found that growth enhancements are modest and a 10% increase in relative growth rate can translate to a much higher relative growth rate in the early exponential phases of plant growth. Kirschbaum suggests that genetic manipulation of photosynthesis should include appropriate crop management and close examination of plant attributes to maximize photosynthetic enhancement.

Conclusions

In the studies of C_3 plant species, increases in CO_2 and temperature often increased the rate of photosynthesis and biomass production. In warm weather C_4 plants, increases in CO_2 often offset the deleterious effects of increased temperature, resulting in no significant changes in overall biomass. It is possible that C_3 plants may have an advantage in future elevated CO_2 and increased temperature conditions. Along with increases in overall growth, seed production and quality is a key issue related to the response of C_3 plants to increased

CO_2. Nitrogen limitation is vital to understanding changes in seed production and increased nitrogen acquisition or decreased nitrogen concentration often leads to increased seed production, especially in legume nitrogen-fixing species. Decreases in nitrogen concentration may not decrease seed quality if nitrogen concentration is reduced in the albumen, not the embryo.

Examining soil dynamics, increased CO_2 environments often lead to increases in belowground carbon flux, nitrogen uptake and overall plant productivity, leading to long-term forest enrichment. However, in other geographic areas, increased CO_2 may lead to increases in N_2O and CH_4 in uplands and wetlands respectively, negating the positive effects of CO_2 enrichment by stimulating production of potent greenhouse gases. Forests sequester large amounts of carbon from our atmosphere, but deforestation is contributing negatively to this effect, accounting for losses of potential carbon sinks. Despite their substantial ability to sequester atmospheric carbon, we cannot solely rely on forests to absorb the risks of increasing anthropogenic sources of carbon.

In modern agriculture, the exogenous-toxin quantities produced by transgenic Bt cotton and rice significantly decreases in different parts of each plant under increased CO_2 conditions. Respective pests accordingly fed on the reduced toxin parts of each plant, however increases in CO_2 also lead to decreased overall pupal and larval weight of pests, suggesting that Bt cotton and rice crops are not under serious risk of reduced efficiency in increased CO_2 environments.

Overall, increases in CO_2 often lead to increased plant efficiency, photosynthesis, and seed and biomass production, but the magnitude of these increases is significantly dependent on other limiting factors such as carbon sink capabilities and nitrogen availability. Plants will only be able to positively respond to CO_2 increases as much as their genetic capacity allows. Also, increases in biomass under elevated CO_2 conditions may lead to short-term gains for plants, but could lead to long-term inefficiencies. There is significant potential for future studies of the effect of increased CO_2 on agricultural productivity and these studies might contain extensions of current research relating to seed quality, long-term effects, and specific crops vital to the global community.

References Cited

Chen, F., Wu, G., Ge, F., Parajulee, M. N., 2011. Relationships between exogenous-toxin quantity and increased biomass of transgenic Bt crops under elevated carbon dioxide. Ecotoxicology and Environmental Safety 74, 1074–1080.

Cure, J. D., Acock, B., 1986. Crop Responses to Carbon Dioxide Doubling: A Literature Survey. Agricultural and Forest Meteorology 38, 127–145.

Drake, J. E., Gallet-Budynek, A., Hofmockel, K. S., Bernhardt, E. S., Billings, S. A., Jackson, R. B., Johnsen., K. S., Lichter, J., McCarthy, H. R., McCormack, M. L., Moore, D. J. P., Oren, R., Palmroth, S., Phillips, R. P., Pippen, J. S., Pritchard, S. G., Treseder, K. K., Schlesinger, W. H., DeLucia, E. H., Finzi, A. C., 2011. Increases in the flux of carbon belowground stimulate nitrogen uptake and sustain the long-term enhancement of forest productivity under elevated CO_2. Ecology Letters 14, 348–357.

Frenk, G., Van der Linden, L., Mikkelsen, T. N., Brix, H., Jorgensen, R. B., 2011. Increased [CO_2] does not compensate for negative effects on yield caused by higher temperature and [O_3] in *Brassica napus* L. European Journal of Agronomy 35, 127–134.

Fuhrer, J., 2003. Agroecosystem responses to combinations of elevated CO_2, ozone, and global climate change. Agriculture, Ecosystems and Environment 97, 1–20.

Hikosaka, K., Kinugasa, T., Oikawa, S., Onoda, Y., Hirose, T., 2011. Effects of elevated CO_2 concentration on seed production in C_3 annual plants. Experimental Botany 62, 1523–1530.

Kirschbaum, M.U.F., 2011. Does Enhanced Photosynthesis Enhance Growth? Lessons Learned from CO_2 Enrichment Studies. Plant Physiology 155, 117–124.

Leakey, A. D. B., Uribelarrea, M., Ainsworth, E. A., Naidu, S. L., Rogers, A., Ort, D. R., Long, S. P., 2006. Photosynthesis, Productivity, and Yield of Maize Are Not Affected by Open-Air Elevation of CO_2 Concentration in the Absence of Drought. Plant Physiology 140, 779-790.

Lee, J. S., 2011. Combined effect of elevated CO_2 and temperature on the growth and phenology of two annual C_3 and C_4 weedy species. Agriculture, Ecosystems and Environment 140, 484–491.

Morgan, J., LeCain, D., Pendall, E., Blumenthal, D., Kimball, B., Carrillo, Y., Williams, D., Heisler-White, J., Dijkstra, F., West., M., 2011. C_4 grasses prosper as carbon dioxide eliminates desiccation in warm semi-arid grassland. Nature 476, 10274–10279.

Pan, Y., Birdsey, R. A., Fang, J., Houghton, R., Kauppi, P. E., Kurz, W. A., Phillips, O. L., Shvidenko, A., Lewis, S. L., Canadell, J. G., Ciais, P., Jackson, R. B., Pacala, S. W., McGuire, A. D., Piao, S., Rautiainen, A., Sitch, S., Hayes, D., 2011. A Large and Persistent Carbon Sink in the World's Forests. Science 333, 988–993.

Rosenberg, N. J., 1981. The Increasing CO_2 Concentration in the Atmosphere and its Implication on Agricultural Productivity. Climate Change 3, 265–279.

Rosenberg, N. J., 1982. The Increasing CO_2 Concentration in the Atmosphere and its Implication on Agricultural Productivity II. Effects Through CO_2-Induced Climatic Change. Climate Change 4, 239–254.

Van Groenigen, K. J., Osenberg, C. W., Hungate, B. A., 2011. Increased soil emissions of potent greenhouse gases under increased atmospheric CO_2. Nature 475, 214–216.

3. Bridging the Gap: Climatological Effects on Marine Capture Fisheries

Alyshia M. Silva

Climate change in marine ecosystems is a broad and inclusive matter; understanding its synergistic effects on both the marine world and human world is crucial to taking the next steps of reducing the uncertainties of climate impacts while creating adaptive, resilient ecosystems that can benefit both social-environmental systems. The following essays review data regarding climate change and its effects on marine wild capture fisheries. The marine world has become a forgotten landscape to society, especially when simple measures can be put into place to deter overexploitation of our capture fisheries. One of the greatest threats to global marine biodiversity is the overexploitation of bycatch and can be efficiently resolved by simply identifying and changing gear technology. Even fishing low-trophic level (LTL) species, which make up the largest proportion of biomass in an ecosystem, at conventional maximum sustainable yield (MSY) can have large impacts on the ecosystem. MSY itself is coming under great scrutiny although it was once a coveted solution to overexploitation, resulting in maximum economic yield becoming more popularized for its benefits to society in the long-term.

Now more than ever we are bridging the gap between localized anthropogenic and environmental pressures, using a diverse array of models in helping policy-makers and fishermen answer real-life, complex fishery issues. Studies are now integrating models for better

91

interdisciplinary results, one such being the development of bio-economic models (BEMs) so as to act as tools for policy-makers and fishermen to understand the feedback effects between human activity and natural resource dynamics.

Another important feature of marine capture fisheries is the lack of global standardization. As seen in the Azores fleet, small- and large-scale fisheries are significantly different in the scale of operation, employment generation, and degree of capital intensity and investment. However, there is much debate over what exactly is large- and small-scale because there is no universal definition for these types of operations nor are there boundaries where one sector ends and the other begins. As well, little attention is given to the amount of uncertainty in projecting spatial distributions of marine populations.

Developing sustainable marine capture models to protect the non-human ecosystem is no longer enough. Newer studies show that human beings are indeed a part of the biological world and creating sustainability is not only needed for marine populations but for human beings themselves. Marine capture fisheries produce 82 million tonnes of fish a year and may have now reached up to 100 million tons, a possible upper limit. While demand is high, marine populations are highly stressed by excessive fishing pressure, toxic contamination, pollution, costal degradation, and climate change. How fisheries are governed and the success of related international and national policy will play a crucial role in ensuring that marine capture fisheries continue feeding the world. To save ourselves we must indeed save the world.

Climate Change and Marine Capture Fisheries

R.I. Perry's paper *Potential impacts of climate change on marine wild capture fisheries* published in the Journal of Agricultural Science (Perry 2011) reviews data regarding climate change and its effects on marine wild capture fisheries. Climate change in marine ecosystems is a broad and inclusive matter; understanding its synergistic effects on both the marine world and human world is crucial to taking the next steps of reducing the uncertainties of climate impacts while creating adaptive, resilient ecosystems that can benefit both social-environmental systems.

About 20% of the world's population relies on marine wildlife capture as a means of subsistence—a factor in much of the developing world's economy—and for jobs in the marketing and processing sectors. However, due to growing pressures ranging from human to environmental stressors, the ability of marine ecosystems to continue meet the world's needs is becoming questionable.

Many studies have shown that climate change is directly affecting fish abundance and location. The warming of waters near the equator causes a shift in marine populations pole-ward, encouraging their seasonal migrations sooner and for longer periods of time, while moving them away from historical fishing grounds.

Using a range of physical conditions, modeling studies have projected ranges shifts of 45–60 km per decade. Using a high CO_2 emission scenario, an estimated 80% of species will move towards the poles, resulting in local extinctions of fish in sub-polar, tropical, and semi-enclosed bodies of water. Overall, however, little change in global maximum catch potential will occur, meaning higher-latitude areas will increase on average 30–70%, while the average of the tropics dropped to 40%. It is developing countries nearer to the equator that will be most harmed by the pole-ward shift of fish population while developed countries to the north will benefit from increased fish populations. The low-emission scenario produced less clear results, but in a similar nature.

Primary production within marine ecosystems plays a vital, yet at times confusing, role within climate change modeling systems. Coupling complex food webs (predator and competitor interactions), biology, and physics, model formulations of increased primary production led to unexpected declines in more abundant catches and increased populations for some threatened species.

Declines of phytoplankton biomass in eight out of the ten oceans were attributed to increasing sea surface temperatures and observational increases in surface air temperatures of 6°C over the past 50 years is leading to loss of perennial ice, coral bleaching, retreating glaciers, and a net decrease of primary production.

Zooplankton play a crucial role within the marine ecosystem, shifting their range to a greater extent and faster than any other marine or terrestrial group. Within an experimental and simplified marine food web that included both zooplankton and phytoplankton, increased temperatures led to blooms of zooplankton and decreases in primary productivity of phytoplankton. This led to an overall decrease in marine biomass; these studies conclude that even small temperature shifts can lead to huge impacts on the ecosystem.

The combined pressures of fishing for an increasingly demanding human population and global climate change appear to be too much for the marine ecosystem to adequately recover from. The potential costs of adapting to a 2°C warmer world by 2050 include estimated global losses in landed catch value of $7–$19 billion for developing nations and $2–$8 billion for the developed world.

Climate change will have a direct impact on marine ecosystems, food security, economics, and politics. Climate change and its effects will directly negatively impact the developing world while possibly benefitting the developed world, a problem of environmental justice. To better handle the currently stressed marine world we must couple social-ecological systems to develop a resilient yet adaptive human and ecological system that can adequately respond swiftly and effectively.

Bycatch Governance and Best Practice Mitigation Technology in Global Tuna Fisheries

One of the greatest threats to global marine biodiversity is the overexploitation of bycatch and target species in marine capture fisheries. The primary mortality sources of bycatch, as well as other linked species like seabirds, sea turtles, marine mammals, and sharks, are due to the purse seine and pelagic longline tuna fisheries. Substantial progress is being made at identifying gear technology solutions but more comprehensive consideration is necessary to identify conflicts and mutual benefits from mitigation methods. There is a lack of performance standards along with inadequate observer coverage for all oceanic purse seiners and incomplete data collection, all of which hinder assessing measures efficacy.

Underneath the large umbrella of state laws and international codes of conduct, States and ocean users develop and apply environmentally safe and selective fishing gear practices to maintain biodiversity, structure, processes, and services. These practices are meant to minimize waste and bycatch, bycatch being defined as retained catch of non-targeted fish, discarded catch, and unobserved mortalities. Bycatch may contain a variety of different species which are critical to maintaining the function and structure of the ecosystem as well as the continued provision of services provided by the ecosystem.

Bycatch and its overexploitation is the largest driver in the change and loss of marine biodiversity, primarily affecting k-selective species, species with sporadic recruitment, and even species with high fecundity. In 1992–2001, averages of 7.3 million tons of fish were discarded annually, presenting 8% of the world catch. Marine capture fisheries have negatively affected genetic diversity and environmental integrity, altering the distribution of fish size and reducing reproductive potential, possibly changing the evolutionary characteristics of populations. Unsustainable bycatch fishing mortality of some species, in particular if they are keystone or foundation species, can cause extinction cascades, alter trophic interactions, simplify food webs, and change the overall functionality and structure of the system. This directly affects the economic side of fisheries, adversely affecting future catch levels and resulting in allocation issues between fisheries.

Most tuna stocks are fully exploited, overfished, or depleted, as a result of use of purse seine, pelagic longline, and pole-and-line fisheries. At the moment, it is not possible to sustainably increase catches of stock without increasing bycatch levels, chiefly of sea turtles, seabirds, marine mammals, sharks, and juvenile and unmarketable finfish in pelagic and purse seine fisheries. There are multitudes of ways of mitigating bycatch via gear technology, including ways that are specific to area as well as species. To reduce bycatch of birds fishermen should avoid peak periods of bird foraging, reduce detection of bait by dyeing it blue, and limit bird access to baited hooks through underwater setting devices. Using "weak" circle hooks, large whole fish bait instead of squid, setting gear deeper and avoiding hotspots can minimize bycatch of sea turtles, sharks, and marine mammals.

Fishermen themselves must be tapped into for their local knowledge to find effective and practical fishery-specific bycatch solutions. Participation from these fishermen could also lead to the fishing industry themselves developing a sense of ownership for bycatch reduction methods. Methods that are shown to minimize, reduce interactions with, and offset mortality of bycatch should be implemented if they are practical, safe, and economically viable or beneficial. Also, most importantly, a viable mitigation method will not increase bycatch of other unwanted bycatch species or sizes.

Five tuna Regional Fishery Management Organizations (RFMOs) were established to manage global fisheries for tuna and tuna-like species; the Commission for the Conservation of Southern Bluefin Tuna (CCBST), Indian Ocean Commission (IOTC), Inter-American Tropical Tuna Commission (IATTC), International Commission for the Conservation of Atlantic Tunas (ICCAT), and Western and Central Specific Fisheries Commission (WCPFC). All except for IATTC had binding measures on longline sea-bird bycatch; IOTC, ITAAC, and WCPFC require gear technology methods to mitigate turtle bycatch in purse seine fisheries ; IOTC, ITAAC, ICCAT, and WCPFC restrict shark finning practices and prohibit the retention of thresher shark species; all except CCBST have adopted legally binding measures to mitigate the bycatch of juvenile/small tunas and other unmarketable species; and only ITAAC have quantifiable performance standards.

There is also a need for observer data collection, of which only two organizations, IATTC and WCPFC, have close to 100% observer coverage. To support robust assessments of bycatch there must be substantial increases in bycatch data collection, employment of standardized monitoring, open access to regional- and national-level observer program datasets, and determination of how individual datasets can be incorporated.

Illegal, unreported, and unregulated (IUU) tuna fishing further exacerbates overexploitation of bycatch, reaching an annual value of $581 million, the illegal proportion of total tuna landings estimated to be a total of 5%. ICCAT, CCSBT, and IATTC have adopted documentation schemes which are generally unsuccessful in deterring IUU fishing due to weaknesses of corruption, inadequate laws, lack of resources for surveillance, and mis-labeling of seafood.

The overexploitation of tuna and tuna bycatch can be attributed to tuna-RFMO's inability to fully adopt conservation and management measures via consensus-based decision-making and ability for members to opt out of adopted measures. This is exacerbated by conflicting objectives of distant fishing nations that wish to maintain their dominance and control of fishing populations. This prevents RFMOs from adopting best practice methods as well as resulting in low compliance by Member States. Commercial viable changes in gear technology and methods can in fact reduce nearly all tuna bycatch in tuna fisheries to nominal levels. These methods include voluntary initiatives such as input and output controls, fleet communication, and industry self-policing.

Impacts of Fishing Low-Trophic Level Species on Marine Ecosystems

Smith et al. (2011) explored the effects of fishing on low-trophic level (LTL) species. They concluded that fishing these LTL species at conventional maximum sustainable yield (MSY) levels can have large impacts on the ecosystem, especially when they constituted a high proportion of the biomass in the ecosystem. They also concluded that halving exploitation rates would result in lower impacts on the marine ecosystem while maintaining 80% of MSY.

Concern has risen over the effects of fishing on the structure and function of marine ecosystems, particularly LTL species because a majority of them are plankton feeders. LTL species, which include anchovies, sardines, herrings, mackerel, krill, and capelin, are found in high abundance in schools or aggregations and account for 30% of global fisheries production.

LTL species are the principle means of transferring energy from plankton to larger predatory fish and upwards to marine mammals and seabirds. Indirectly, seabirds, whales, and high- trophic level (HTL) species are affected by the maximum yield of LTL species.

To examine and summarize the broader effects of fishing LTL species, five-well studied ecosystem regions were modeled. These regions included the California current, northern Humboldt, North Sea, southern Benguela, and southeast Australia. For each ecosystem and model, five LTL species or groups were subjected to a range of fishing pressures which resulted in depletion levels relative to unfished biomass from zero to 100%. Impacts on other species within the ecosystem were measured relative to biomass levels of unfished focal LTL populations and all other groups that were fished at current levels.

Widespread impacts of harvesting LTL species were found across the ecosystems and the LTL species that were selected. The percentage of affected species increased with the level of depletion of the LTL species, but the exact extent of the impacts varied across LTL species. Impacts were both positive and negative, and at times, counter-intuitive considering that there were severe impacts with low depletion levels. Negative impacts were felt by marine mammals, seabirds, and commercial species, although the majority of these impacts were very small.

Overall, harvesting LTL species was found to have high impacts, although the species with high impacts were not consistent across all ecosystems. Management implications then vary geographically; large impacts may require a change in overall harvest levels whereas LTL species with small impacts could be harvested at conventional levels. The range of impacts could be explained by the relative abundance of the group in the ecosystem, the trophic level of the group, and the connectivity of the group in the food web.

Wider implications of exploitation of LTL species include the tension between global food security and the protection of biodiversity. Lower exploitation rates can cause smaller impacts on the ecosystem but also sustain lower yield rates. Lower impacts can be achieved by lowering the MSY exploitation levels to a target of 75% unexploited biomass for an LTL species. This will cost less than 20% of long-term yield, implying lower fishing effort but long-term economic optimum levels. This study supports the ongoing substantial yields of LTL species while achieving ecological objectives in the face of feeding the global population.

Net Economic Effects of Achieving Maximum Sustainable Yield in Fisheries

Increasing the economic performance of marine capture fisheries is becoming an increasingly important management strategy, specifically using the maximum economic yield (MEY). Critics of MEY state that reducing the level of fishing necessary to achieve the target MEY will result in a subsequent loss of economic activity elsewhere in the economy. Using an input-output framework within a bioeconomic model, the net economic effects of achieving MEY were calculated for short- and long-term performances when moving towards MEY. Overall losses were felt by the community in the short-term while achieving MEY, but achieving MEY was found to be beneficial to the larger society in the long-term.

Relying on economic instruments, key management strategies for fisheries are done by maximizing economic efficiency. This is done through the maximum economic yield (MEY), as defined as "the sustainable catch or effort level for a commercial fishery that allows net economic returns to be maximized". The short and long term effects of achieving MEY in four Australian fisheries is estimated using input-output modeling framework.

Although MEY is a yield or specific level of output, it is also a concept which can be constructed in a multitude of ways. Different than maximum sustainable yield (MSY), MEY requires both input and output simultaneously to determine economically optimal levels. MSY can result in yields similar to MEY, but only one such combination of input and output can result in MEY. MEY can vary depending upon catch, size, and effort but can be defined as the combination of both effort and output and the capitalization of both revenue and cost curves.

Most fisheries are characterized by a number of fishing systems for a large variety of catch and MEY suggests that fleet reductions in excess of 50% may be necessary to maximize economic profits. Achieving MEY will most likely be accompanied by reduction in employment and the total income of the crew declining (dependent on the payment system), while the individualized income of the crew member will increase. Fishing at MEY reduces the number of vessels on the ocean to maximize economic efficiency for the remaining vessel owners as well as increase wages of the remaining crew members. In dependent fishing coastal communities, higher incomes will lead to an increased demand for products in the local area, thereby stimulating production, incomes, and employment.

There will also be indirect and direct effects on the intermediary and final demand sectors in the economy–goods and services (e.g., fuel, equipment) and other sectors higher up the economic chain (e.g., processors, retailers). The extent of the impact will depend upon the dependency of these sectors on the domestic fishing industry as well as the level of catches of MEY. The final demand sector, as represented by the purchase of goods and services by consumers, will be affected due to the loss of income from the displaced crew of the closed-down vessels.

The four Australian fisheries that were targeted to reduce overfishing while moving the fishery closer to the target of maximum sustainable yield were the eastern tuna and billfish fishery (ETBF), the southern and eastern scalefish and shark fishery (SESSF), the northern prawn fishery (NPF), and a sector named the gillnet, hook, and trap sector (GHTS). The first three represent two-thirds of the total AU$288 million of all the Commonwealth managed fisheries.

The input-output methodology includes the notion that the production of output requires input and a multiplier effect will occur to ensure the buying and selling of multiple goods and services to maintain the fishing system. Three different types of effects make up the multipliers: the initial (or direct) effect, the production-induced effect, and the consumption-induced effect. The initial effect refers to the initial amount of dollars spent; the production-induced effect is the purchase of extra goods to supply the extra demand; the consumption-induced effect is the proportion of the extra income that will be re-spent on final goods and services within the local economy.

As stated previously, the reduction of fishing effort to achieve MEY will heavily depend upon the existing level of fishing effort, capacity, and stocks. Within the model, fishing fleets of the four fisheries were reduced 45–60%, as a means to reduce overfishing, maintain biological sustainability, and improve economic performance. Initially, this reduced total income and input usage in the economy but the profitability and incomes of the fisheries will increase in the long run when MEY is achieved. The structural adjustment has lowered costs within NPF, ETBF, CTS, and GHTS by, respectively, 27%, 18%, 57%, and 18%, while catches and revenue decreased by, respectively,

15%, 39%, and 5%, while catches increased in ETBF by 3%. Prices for the fish remained unchanged due to prices being driven by world markets and exchange rate fluctuations rather than on quantity of domestic landings.

The net economic impacts are estimated once evaluating the direct effect (wages and profits to the fishery) and the production number and consumption-induced effects. As a long term benefit, the reduction in fleet size increased fishery profits in three of the four sectors, the exception being GHTS. This is an exception due to prices for repair and maintenance, and individualized vessels, rather than the entire section, have an increased profit. This larger loss of labor and reduced capacity explains the larger loss of consumption, a direct negative effect on the fishing community. In the short term, there are overall net economic effects on moving towards MEY, except for ETBF. However, in the long term, the expected rise in catches of MEY is expected to result in a positive national economic effect.

The two main effects of achieving MEY include fleet reductions (an initial change in profits and wages) and changes in revenue. This analysis, overall, ignores the economic effects on the community and little research has been done as to the effects on the displaced crew. Achieving MEY is clearly a challenge in the short run, but poses benefits for the community economically and sustainably by increasing wages for individuals and making environments more resilient in the long term.

A Review of EU Bio-Economics Models for Fisheries: The Value of a Diversity of Models

Fishing activities include an integration of biology and economics, a recent new branch within economics that has resulted in a growing interest and use of bio-economic models (BEM) as tools for policy-makers and fishermen to understand the feedback effects between human activity and natural resource dynamics. Using mathematical representations of biological and economic systems known as bio-economic models (BEM), thirteen of these existing European Union models are presented and reviewed. Used in either the Atlantic Ocean of the Mediterranean Sea, the thirteen models (AHF, BIRDMOD, BEMMFISH, COBAS, ECOCORP, ECONMULT, EIAA, EMMFID, FLR, MEFISTO, MOSES, SRRMCF, and TEMAS) help bridge the gap between localized anthropogenic and environmental pressures. A diverse array of models is useful in helping policy-makers and fishermen answer real-life, complex fishery issues. Presello et al (2011) focuses on how BEMs evaluated anthropogenic and biological interrelated components as well as EU policy surrounding fisheries.

There is an obvious and simple relationship between marine resources and users, extracting and fishing result in fish mortality, which is directly affected by biological components (predators, nutrient availability, etc.) and economic components (management, fuel costs, etc.). The need for BEMs and integrated approaches to sustainable fisheries comes from the fact that both economics and biology play a crucial and interrelated role within marine fisheries. BEM incorporates both biological variability as well as human behavioral traits using system dynamics, interactions and feedback mechanisms, key parameters, and data availability as well as their relationships with each other.

The two classifications of BEM are simulation (what if?) and optimization (what's best?). Simulation models strive to simulate a system of biological and economic components into a scenario to evaluate alternative management strategies or model external variables. In comparison, optimization models are designed to find optimal solutions within a pre-defined objective, such as maximizing revenue, profit, harvest, fleet capacity, welfare, or minimizing day-at-sea costs or ecosystem impacts.

All thirteen of the models that were reviewed except MOSES could conduct simulations, while others models like EIAA,

EMMFID, FLR, and SRRMCF can conduct both simulations and optimizations.

Conclusions from these models are also dependent on input (effort, gear restrictions, area closures) and output (quota, catch, composition, maximum landing size). BIRDMOD, BEMMFISH, COBAS, and MOSES solely model input controlled fisheries while the remaining models use both input and output regulated fisheries.

BEMs are intended to reflect the main features of the fishery under analysis including the fact that different management regimes are in force in different areas for different fisheries. However, many of the features of the models are not specific to regions and fisheries, so some aspects of these models, such as algorithms, are generic. None of the models provide a complete biological overview and some are easily driven by routine settings of single-species or multi-species outputs, recruitment relationships, and growth and maturity. There is a trade-off between the generality and complexity of BEMs. SRRMCF, EIAA, ECONMULT, and EMMFID do not have a biological component whereas other models, such as the FLR and BIRDMOD, have as strengths lie in biological components.

The BEMs' economic components are heterogeneous but rely upon three common mechanisms: fleet and effort dynamics, price dynamics, and cost dynamics. However, approaches to using these mechanisms vary, depending on the purpose of the model, availability of data and their structure, and the features of the fisheries. Optimization or simulation models determine the relevance of the economic component and the approach used for its implementation, especially since both economic and biological data have different availabilities and detail.

Outputs of BEMs are mainly used by policy-makers and it is important that BEM results are standardized and made familiar so that communication between government and fishery experts is at its best. These models are made to assess and compare stocks with sustainable levels with catch capabilities and economic profit, as well as incorporate biological indicators (e.g. sustainable stocks), capacity indicators (e.g. catch capability), economic indicators (short or long term economic goals), and sociological characteristics (e.g. employment), all of which are important to building sustainable fisheries.

The utility of a model depends on the framing of the question being asked. While optimization models consider fixed prices, simulation models adopt elasticity functions to simulate marine dynamics. However, there is room for further integration between biological and economic components, as made clear in the fact that three of the BEMs were purely economic (ECONMULT, EIAA, EMMFID, and SRRMCF) while the remaining nine had both of an economic and biological component. However, all of these models require either economic or biological expertise.

Defining Scale in Fisheries: Small versus Large-Scale Fishing Operations in the Azores

In the North Atlantic, both large- and small-scale fishing operations of the Azorean fishing fleet compete for the same limited resources, fishing grounds, and markets via in the coexistence of both large- and small-scale fishing operations. These two sectors are very different in the scale of operation, employment generation, and degree of capital intensity and investment. However, there is much debate over what exactly is large- and small-scale because there is no universal definition for these types of operations nor are there boundaries where one sector ends and the other beings. These two sectors were compared using policy-relevant data so as to better understand the socio-economic importance, as well as develop future policies based upon a more holistic and ecosystem approach to fisheries management. This comparison of the Azorean fleets showed that the small-scale fisheries were more sustainable overall because of their using less energy, providing more jobs to the community, and supplying fresher food for human consumption with a higher landed value.

There is long-standing assumption that large-scale fisheries are more economical. However, due to declining world catches and fleet over-capacity and overcapitalization it is clear that new policies and strategies are needed. The small-scale fishery was largely ignored in economic calculuations as it was seen as being inefficient and retrogressive and likely to gradually disappear as large-scale fishing expanded. However, small-scale fisheries have withstood and even flourished despite longstanding marginalization. Many studies show that small-scale fisheries are, in fact, sustainable resources which ensure sound policies of employment, income distribution, energy consumption, and product quality. Small-scale fisheries account for anything between one-half to three-quarters of global fish production and employ 50 of the 51 million fishermen.

However, these types of fisheries are poorly documented and provide no insight into future policy largely because there is no uniform structure to the definition of "small-scale". Each individual fishery and community is unique and distinct from others and there are numerous ways to divide fishing fleets into separate sectors. A study was conducted to define the commercial fishing fleet in Azores as small or large using the socially-constructed definition. This included surveys to acquire socio-economic data for the year 2005, surveying vessel owners/skippers, crew members, and auction buyers, resulting in survey of at least 41% of the active fishing vessel population. This compared policy-relevant socioeconomic and environmental parameters, such as revenue, employment, by-catch and discards, and fuel consumption.

The first aspect of this survey defined small- and large-scale fleets using three main steps: (1) define the fishery as gear type/vessel size combination, (2) list gear type/vessel size combinations with their corresponding catch capacity, and (3) develop a cumulative percentage distribution of landed weight. The small- and large-scale is then determined by 50% cut-off of cumulative landed value. When more than one type of gear was used the prevalent gear (responsible for more than 80% of the landings) were used.

The study was based on the active use of 666 vessels, 2,160 fishermen, and live bait captures reaching almost 180 tonnes. The final cut-off point reached 51.6%, corresponding to 63.3% cumulative landed value. The Azorean fleet is traditionally known as a small-scale and sustainable fishery which has replaced larger commercial fisheries. However, it is multi-segmented, targeting multiple species with a wide range of gears and currently exploits 50–60 of the 500 fish species within the ecosystem. More than 90% of the fleet comprises vessels less than 12 meters in length, 25% of which were non-motorized. Thus, the small-scale fishing fleet is dominated by small, old, wooden vessels of low power that on average use 31 kW and weight 3.2 tonnes.

The small-scale sector encompasses 90% of the fishing fleet and employs almost three times more fishermen than its counterpart. It is also less fuel-intensive, consuming half as much fuel per tonne of fish landed, and achieves a higher landed value per tonne. The crew, having smaller landings, also has more time to clean and prepare fish for favorable presentation, fetching higher prices. The average wage of the crew is higher than the minimum wage of alternative employment, however, it is still €250 less for employees of large-scale fisheries.

Thus, small-scale fisheries have the potential to be profitable activities in coastal communities. Not only do they employ more individuals in the North Atlantic, they meet more policy goals, such as catching fish for direct human consumption and deriving a higher economic value from each tonne of fish landed. These fisheries can also maintain marginalized markets, depending less upon foreign and expensive sources of oil.

But there is not as much information about the economics of small-scale fisheries as needed for a full analysis. They should become a top priority in development and research. At the moment they serve as legitimate sources of income, employment, and food security, and development strategies should be encouraged to create synergistic effects between large- and small-scale fisheries.

Uncertainties in Projecting Spatial Distributions of Marine Populations

An important issue for marine ecologists and managers is the projection of future spatial distributions of marine populations. Projecting spatial distributions can be a useful but only if they are given with a known and sufficiently high level of confidence. These uncertainties can arise for the observation process, conceptual and numerical model formulations, parameter estimates, model evaluation, appropriate spatial and temporal scales, and the adaptation of living systems. To analyze different sources of uncertainty and the ways they are considered in current studies, 75 publications for 2005–2009 were selected and the frequency of considered type of uncertainty was calculated. What was found was that there is little attention to many sources of uncertainty except for parameter estimates. Unless certainty can be better accounted for, such projections may be of limited use for managerial purposes.

Spatial distributions define the geographical extent of marine population, as well as the abundance of the individuals or density within these geographical boundaries. Projecting spatial distributions for marine populations is becoming a more difficult task and a chief concern for managers, conservationists, and human communities that depend on marine resources. In particular, measuring uncertainty is important because spatial distributions should only be useful if they are given with a high-level of confidence. Major sources of uncertainty are related to the observation process, conceptual and numerical model formulations, parameter estimates, model evaluation, appropriate spatial and temporal scales, and the adaptation of living systems.

The observation process is the way we perceive the marine world, which is already a very limited methodology due to filtered observation instruments and a lack of a uniform method to observe adequately. Our representation of this world is therefore inadequate and incomplete. Conceptual model formulations are mental representations of the processes that control the spatial distribution of marine populations. These models are becoming increasingly difficult to use because environmental conditions can no longer be compared to observable past climatological phenomenon. Numerical implementations within a conceptual model can represent functional relationships, deal with interactions, non-linearity, and complexity in general, and can accommodate various statistical distributions. However, they do not outperform other methods under every circumstance. A model evaluation provides an objective way of measuring model performance and validation on independent datasets is the most robust approach. Spatial and temporal scales are important to understand the distribution and abundance of organisms and inference will be weaker when based upon vague notions of scale than if precise notion of scale is used. The adaptability of living systems is also highly questionable considering that we have never seen these effects before in the history of human-kind. Predicting future changes based upon past observations is highly uncertain, however, ecosystems are highly adaptive and have a strong dependence on historical contingencies.

The author conducted a literature survey that includes the following words and their variations: spatial, fish, distribution, benth, geography, habitat, sea, ocean, marin, and model. These articles are restricted to a period from 2005 to March 2010 within the fields of marine and freshwater biology, oceanography, and fisheries. Seventy-five articles were then selected that presented models that were used or could be used for the projection of spatial distribution of marine populations. Within each article, uncertainty within the previously mentioned criteria was assessed. Overall, little attention is given to the various sources of uncertainties in models and consequently to uncertainties in the resulting projections. Only 5 of the 75 studies explicitly accounted for the observation process in the model design; conceptual model uncertainty only accounted for one of the studies surveyed; uncertainty in the appropriateness of the numerical formula is addressed in one-fourth of the articles; parameter uncertainty was accounted for in 69%; 45% of the model evaluation was based upon visual comparison of predicted and observed distributions were infrequent; spatial and temporal scales were defined before modeling in 45% of the literature; only 4% discussed possible implications of ecological adaptability for projected changes.

Uncertainty in spatial projections has been poorly considered in marine ecological research, indicating that the current projections in marine biota distributions are likely poorly reliable. There is an explicit trend in handling various sources of uncertainty in model projections but a more extensive study would be required to confirm this. Highly uncertain or inaccurate projections could negatively harm managerial and conservation efforts, erasing what "success" we have created if future studies show that these uncertainties are indeed too great to ignore.

Food Security and Marine Capture Fisheries: Characteristics, Trends, Drivers, and Future Perspectives

In 2006, marine capture fisheries produce 82 million tons of fish a year and may have now reached up to 100 million tons, a possible upper limit. An important source of protein, vitamins, and micronutrients, particularly for low-income populations in rural areas, fisheries, which include 32 million tons from inland aquaculture and 20 million tons from marine aquaculture, play a critical role in global food security. While demand is high, marine populations are highly stressed by excessive fishing pressure, toxic contamination, pollution, costal degradation, and climate change. How fisheries are governed and the success of related international and national policy will play a crucial role in ensuring that marine capture fisheries continue feeding the world.

By 2050, the world's population will reach 9 billion, mostly in the developing world (5.6–7.9 billion). Fishery resources are an important part of the world's daily diet, especially for low-income populations in developing countries. At least 20% of fisheries are moderately exploited while 52% are fully exploited, 19% are overexploited, 8% are depleted, and 1% is recovering from previous depletion. These numbers could lead to the permanent decline of fish populations, leaving the world to solve a significant new food deficit. Other issues of marine capture fisheries include 11–26 million tons of illegal, unreported, and unregulated (IUU) fishing as well as 9.5 million tons of discarded unwanted catch.

Destructive and IUU fishing can cause great environmental harm in itself, especially when resulting in marine debris from lost gear that continue to fish and entangle wildlife. It greatly affects the food web and can alter the ecosystem function and structure while lessening productivity and resilience to other drivers such as climate change.

Fish overall are important as a means of food and livelihood, especially for the poor. At least 1.5 billion people rely on fish as 20% of their average per capita intake of animal protein, the majority of these populations coming from low-income food deficit countries. About 110 million tons of produced fish are used for food directly while 33 million tons are used as fishmeal. Around 42 million people work directly in the fishing sector while related activities support at least 500 million livelihoods. Overall, fisheries and aquaculture sector contribute about 0.5–2.5% of a country gross domestic product (GDP). Poverty within these low-income countries may contribute to over fishing; however, healthy fisheries can contribute to poverty reduction through generation of revenues and wealth-creation.

World population is a key driver in fish demand, and with the rise in population and 70% of this population moving to cities, especially ones near coasts, and demand will rise with increased levels of development and living standards. An increasingly globalized market will increase demand as well, and enhance competition. The governance frameworks adopted at the national, regional, and global levels are intended interact in a "continuous but asynchronous manner (i.e. developing at different speeds in different places)". Weak governance, on the other hand, has become a major problem mostly due to incomplete jurisdictions and the lack of clear and defendable entitlements.

With increasing globalization comes a need to solve issues with an inter-disciplinary focus, dealing with economics, environment, and the human perspective. Global climate change in itself will test not only humanity's ability to reduce consumption and find environmentally sustainable means of fish production, but will test the ecosystem's resilience and ability to adapt. The ecosystem's ability to produce fish, stability of supply, and access to food will be affected by global climate change, and methodologies incorporating both the social and hard sciences will be needed to adequately address these issues.

Although global food security might change minimally, local consequences will be drastic, particularly in poor coastal areas. A reduction of harvesting capacity will result in consequences for both humans and the environment and we need to address key interconnected global/local issues to smartly use our resources. Without key governance building, fishery resources will drop. We must look to maintain and optimize current production and profitability in terms of quality and quantity. The fishing industry will need, with the help of government, to adapt its technology to changing resources and to support small fisheries that would otherwise create disenfranchised coastal communities. Fisheries governance is a unique combination of public, private, and hybrid institutions and utilizing these administrators is crucial to creating a holistic, multi-disciplinary solution for both people and place.

Summing up Sendai: Progress Integrating Climate Change Science and Fisheries

The Sendai Conference promotes global stabilization and understanding of international waters and inter-related events by pointing out what needs to be improved upon and the successes we have witnessed thus far. Overwhelming evidence was presented at the Sendai Conference of the instability of marine fisheries caused by climate-dependent factors, which include productivity, spatial distribution, phenology, and human dimensions. Not all changes within these factors may be negative but they provide little certainty of how society will adapt.

Control of overfishing has become a global priority to ensure food security, and the Sendai Conference placed a global focus on dealing with the issues, rather than specific regions, species, or other subsets within climate change. Using meta-analyses is becoming a reality with coupled modeling, nesting atmosphere, land, ocean, and other biological components together, and methodologies and models are improving quickly. Methods that bring together regional downscaling (atmospheric models linked to terrestrial and aquatic ecosystems) and upscaling (oceanographic models nested in atmospheric models) are a new development that can provide holistic data and ways to deal with it.

In particular with downscaling, there are no standardized methods and approaches do not exist. Instead, different methodologies for projecting regional and local climates are used and more consistent frameworks are needed. Most studies to date have operated on a species-by-species basis and the lack of species interactions is a clear flaw of these studies. Integrating trophic dynamics through foodweb analyses and size-based methods must become incorporated into existing methodologies as a feasible path to sustainability. There is also great bias towards certain areas where fisheries are examined, such as the North Atlantic, North Pacific, southern Africa, and a few other places globally. We must identify other pertinent climate "hotspots" and focus our attention there as well, whether they be locations that are not well-studied or vulnerable locations that may not exhibit extreme temperature increases.

The effects of climate change become confounded by both additive and multiplicative factors and interactions, worsening issues of marine fisheries. Holistic data through the sciences, social sciences, and policy must come together to understand the synergistic effects, and coupling multi-sectoral models are needed to understand ecosystem and community effects. The issue itself branches across multiple disciplines and will affect all societies but in, perhaps, different ways considering that access to science and technology is not equal and significant latitudinal responses will occur, allowing certain places to adapt more readily than others.

It is also key to understand the direct role humans play within this system, especially because of the economic and regulatory environment fisheries are in. Discussions at Sendai encouraged knowledge from all different types of people and places, therefore exploring diverse perceptions and increase communication among various societal groups. With this information, we can perhaps explore the positive economic effects of other countries, considering that productivity will shift pole-wards.

There are also clear issues between fisheries and climate change specialists— fishery decision-makers are primarily focused on short-term goals while climate change specialists' focus is upon long-term changes. The time-scale solution lies in better communicating the climate-fishery impacts of actions to both parties. The ecosystem approach, an integrated method, encourages society to deal with highly complex issues, especially in a global context.

Conclusions

Throughout our readings we have come across a greater connection between the natural world and the world human beings have created. It is also critical to realize the interconnectedness of economics, politics, society, and biology. To be better equipped to resolving the issues of marine capture fisheries, cooperation among oceanographers, fishery biologists, ecologists, and social scientists is the critical issues – it is the basic interconnectedness of both of the world around us and our society. Through a multitude of ways, marine capture fisheries can become sustainable and profitable, models that nourish not only our bodies but our communities around us. By focusing on global trends and acting locally marine capture fisheries can become resilient ecosystems and economic models globally. Yet, it is important to note that there is still much more research necessary to promote sustainable marine capture fisheries, ones that work with the environment for the betterment of our political economy.

References Cited

Carvalho, N., Edwards-Jones, G., Isidro E. 2011. Defining scale in fisheries: Small versus large-scale fishing operations in the Azores. Fisheries Research 109, 360–369.

Garcia, S.M., Rosenberg, A.A., 2010. Food Security and Marine Capture Fisheries: Characteristics, Trends, Drivers, and Future Perspectives. Philosophical Transitions of the Royal Society 365, 2869–2880.

Gilman, E.L. 2011. Bycatch governance and best practice mitigation technology in global tuna fisheries, Marine Policy 35, 590–509.

Murawski, S.A. 2011. Summing up Sendai: Progress Integrating Climate Change Science and Fisheries. ICES Journal of Marine Science 68, 1368–1372.

Norman-Lopez, A., Pascoe, S. 2011. Net economic effects of achieving maximum sustain yield in fisheries. Marine Policy 35, 489–495.

Perry R. 2010. Potential impacts of climate change on marine wild capture fisheries: an update. The Journal of Agricultural Science 149 63–75.

Planque, B., Bellier E., Loots, C. 2011. Uncertainties in Projecting Spatial Distributions of Marine Populations. ICES Journal of Marine Science 68, 1045–1050.

R. Prellezo, P. Accadia, J. Anderson, B. Anderson, E. Buisman, A. Little, J. Nielson, Jan Poos, J. Powell, C. Rockmann. 2011. A review of EU bio-economic models for fisheries: The value of a diversity of models. Marine Policy 36, 423–431

Smith, A., Brown, C., Bulman, C., Fulton, E., Johnson, P., Kaplan, I., Lozano-Montes, H., Mackinson, S., Marzloff, M., Shannon, L., Shin Y.J., Tam, J. 2011. Impacts of Fishing Low-Trophic Level Species on Marine Ecosystems. Science 6046, 1147–1150

4. Biodoversity in a Changing Climate and Under Human Influences

Mathew Harreld

Perhaps one of the most worrying aspects of a changing climate and growing human influence within that climate is the changes being made to global biodiversity. In the papers summarized below, I discovered that biodiversity is an extremely fragile part of our planet, and it is being upset. Just how much it is being upset I am not sure, and no one is. It is clear, however, how drastically human practices have affected global biodiversity. I have discovered that agriculture and logging are the two largest causes of biodiversity loss. As our population continues to grow so does our need for food and resources. It seems that our immediate action is to use up more land and cut down more trees. From what I have read, and what I have highlighted in my choice of journal articles, is that there is little to no need for this kind of behavior on our part. It appears that biodiversity preservation and farm yield have almost no effect on each other, meaning we can pursue high yield growths and high biodiversity together. In addition, genetically modified crops are one of the best things humans have done to preserve biodiversity. One of the keys to understanding how our current climate and our society affect biodiversity is learning how species have developed throughout history. One of my favorite papers looked at the development of the Amazon rainforest over the past ten to hundred million years. The progression of time, climate, and life is truly remarkable.

The papers that I reviewed are focused on the most recent understanding of how biodiversity has changed over time, how we are changing it currently, how to better understand it, and how we can preserve it. Personally, some of the questions I would recommend to keep in mind are: What is driving these changes in biodiversity? Why? Is it a bad thing? How will it affect our world? Are some of these concerns overblown? Will life continue given the worst-case scenario?

Estimated Extinction Risks of Species by 2100 due to Climate Change

We are currently facing high extinction risks in the near future, and it is becoming essential to understand how and why. First, however, we have to understand the amount of extinction we might be facing. Maclean and Wilson (2011) make these first steps by taking 318 of the top scientific papers on biodiversity loss and calibrating extinction risks, using the International Union for Conservation of Nature's criteria. Their findings suggest declines of up to 14% of species by 2100. Their results also uncover a bias in research; the lack of data from tropical regions of the world, and non-coral marine ecosystems are contributing to incorrect estimates of extinction risks. There is also a gap in our understanding of the effects of climate change on invertebrates, particularly insects. Maclean and Wilson provide a start for quantitatively understanding the risks we are facing in biodiversity loss, and make clear the need for more work to be done.

The recent studies on the effects of climate change on biodiversity appear to be pointing toward great losses of species, some going as far as predicting the next great mass extinction. Many studies released are citing the losses of a particular species that are predicted to occur 2050 and 2100. Other papers are focused on the observable changes in species' environments and their decline rates. But and how accurate are they? This is the question Maclean and Wilson set out to answer.

The authors took the top ten scientific journals dealing with effects of climate change, choosing 130 papers that covered observed and ecological responses of species to climate change and 188 papers that covered predicted ones. The papers thus contained data on extinction risks, population changes, and geographic range changes of 305 different species. MacLean and Wilson then used the International Union for Conservation of Nature (IUCN) Red List Criteria to determine estimates for extinction risks for each species. Using the IUCN method gives universal and comparable data, rather than the individual studies' own derived answers. The authors took into account a variety of possible biases from each individual study, and then compared the results by averaging them across all studies. To remove the bias of closely related species appearing to act similarly because of genetics, the authors created a phylogenetic tree and averaged out the branches and tips to remove any possible discrepancy. The model also took into account spatial patterns in extinctions to avoid a bias in the studies done in regions where species are more at risk of climate change. And lastly, the authors broke up the studies by taxonomic groups (plant, invertebrate, and vertebrate), as well as major ecoregions (i.e. polar, temperate, tropical, marine).

The model utilized research based both on predicted mortality and observed mortality; for studies in which the mortality was based on predictions, 7.69% of species would be threatened by 2100, and for mortalities based on observations, 37.1% would be threatened by 2100. Species more than likely to go extinct by 2100 are 1.9% based on predictions and 12.0% based on observations. The large range between the predicted and observed extinctions is explained by the where the study was done and on what species were observed. A majority of the observational papers were done on land, focusing on rainfall and temperature changes, whereas the prediction papers were done on sea ice changes and ocean circulation changes which produced much higher extinction risks, but there were many fewer of these papers. The authors suggest more studies done on oceanic circulation and acidity changes would result in much better understanding of possible extinction risks. The results also suggest that there seems to be a slight exaggeration on observational data because of a focus on threatened species. The adjustment for spatial patterns in extinctions increased the predicted risk to 10.3%, compared to a 13.9% in observed after adjustments to phylogenetic independence, suggesting that current models are not fully taking into account regions under higher levels of threat to climate change.

The results for the ecoregions suggest that species at higher latitudes are most threatened, as are marine species. The authors also suggest that in the marine environment there is a bias to study to corals, which might be greatly increasing the marine extinction risk. The overall threat of biodiversity changes due to climate change would be better understood by more research in the tropics, as this is where most species exist, and where they seem least threatened by climate change.

Though these results shed much light into the risk biodiversity faces today, it is still important to remember that they are simply estimates that need to be worked on further. First, the IUCN model for categorizing extinction risk is not perfect, as it is extremely difficult to determine the thresholds between criteria, especially when trying to apply it to all species. Also, there was a low risk calculated for invertebrates, but this is most likely due to a lack of knowledge. Most of the data recorded for invertebrate extinction risk came from Lepidoptera, and little research has been done on other insects and the effect climate change might have on them. The results of this paper provide more evidence that anthropologic climate change is one of the major factors leading to extinctions, furthering our need in understanding our impact on our planet. Maclean and Wilson clearly quantify the risk of biodiversity loss, while also highlighting areas of further research. In order to have a better understanding of the loss of biodiversity we might face there must be more studies done on less at-risk species, marine species, subtropical and tropical areas, and invertebrates.

Redesigning and Improving Climate Change Models to Better Show the Impact on Global Environments and Species

Our understanding of how climate change might affect our planet, the ecosystems on it, and the species within them is dependent on computerized climate ecological models. The accuracy of these models is constantly being improved, and here McMahon *et al.* (2011) suggest further fixes that could be made to our current modeling programs. The models are dependent on the data gathered in the field, and therefore the authors suggest a unified method of data gathering, as well as a single database to access all the currently gathered data. From there tweaks, adjustments, and wholesale changes need to be made to various models. Some models will benefit from the greater level of accessible and new field data, and others need to be redesigned. Often a model needs to be made larger and more specific, allowing scientists to more accurately take into account all of the potential shifts and changes of climate, the environment, and of species and their interactions. McMahon *et al.* highlight the five largest gaps in our current models, suggesting how to fix them and how it will benefit us now and in the future.

Species and ecosystems response to climate change is key to our understanding to our environments, and to formulating the best conservation efforts for those environments. Discovering and understanding these responses can only be accomplished through modeling. Modeling allows for simulations of species and ecosystem responses to various changes of climate, but the models are far from perfect. As the authors point out, however, models are constantly being updated and reinvented to improve results. Accurate models would allow a greater understanding of earth systems, and how climate change might affect them. McMahon *et al.* discuss five gaps and ten potential fixes to modeling, as well as creating a internet-based connection between all scientists, so models can be shared and updated seamlessly.

The first gap identified by McMahon *et al.* is the necessity to improve global biodiversity monitoring. The two goals of biodiversity monitoring, as specified by the authors, are to create a baseline of data for natural species levels and estimate the rate of change in biodiversity, and to determine the causes behind the changes. The authors then suggest preexisting biodiversity monitoring sites in Europe and North America, specifically The Smithsonian Institution Global Earth Observatory, as models for future monitoring sites. There is a need for more monitoring sites, but more importantly there is a need for these sites to work together to target potentially at risk areas, and then share these data across the globe. This requires a standardization of procedures to create a simplified system of data sharing amongst researches..

The second gap highlighted is the ability to quantify how sensitive a species is to climate change. Climate can greatly affect species in many ways; climate change could result in extinctions, migrations, range contractions or expansions, or various other effects. To understand and predict these responses to climate change, models must be used. Traditionally scientists have relied on climate envelope models (CEMs) to calculate these changes, but McMahon *et al.* believe a new approach may be required. The limitation of CEMs is that they treat species as non-adaptive to the changes of other species, as well as disregarding temporal climate variability and CO_2 fertilization. Therefore McMahon *et al.* suggest using process-based models to derive these predictions in the future. The main limitation of these models is that they require more data about individual species, and more data on how they interact with other species in their ecosystem.

How full communities of species and how biodiversity as a whole will be affected by climate change is a weak spot in the modeling as well. Mahon *et al.* suggest that in order to model how climate change will affect species-species relationships, modelers must look at the palaeoecological evidence. A new model that combines life-history changes over time, using the palaeoecological evidence, and how they are affected by different climates may allow for a better understanding to how species relationships will change under a changing environment.

The forth gap highlighted by the authors is how to model the influence of genetic variability and adaptive tendencies of species in climate change. Sexually reproducing species have a great variety of genetic information, and this allows for a great variation of possible responses to environmental changes. The ability to adapt to a rapid climate shift is dependent on the plasticity of species, which is related to the range of phenotypes that a species can generate from one genotype, and the greater the plasticity the greater the species' ability to adapt to climate changes. This generic variation could have a huge affect on ecosystems and which species survive climate changes, yet this information is rarely used in the building of models. Mahon *et al.* suggest using already-established data, along with calculated data and laboratory tests of species under specific climate stresses, to develop a unified information base that can be applied in future models. The authors note that there is some use of mathematical integration for population genetics and phylogenetics to determine the short-term and long-term responses of species and populations to climate change.

The final gap stressed by the authors is the necessity to improve the way global models define groupings of plant species. Models currently generate vegetation shifts by using plant functional types, which is a grouping of similar plant species that will most likely adapt in a similar manner. However, using plant functional types comes at the cost of generalized, and sometimes useless data. The authors suggests designing plant functional types around species that are known to be key in ecological function or are extremely responsive to certain climate changes. There is a need for more robust groupings to establish more concrete results, however there also needs to be a way to successfully quantify these data. In the past there was an issue with data availability, but now the global trait databases (GLOPNET) allow access to increasing amounts of data. Further studies will have to be done on plant traits and how they relate to key environmental factors, as well as expanding the current databases of plant traits. McMahon *et al.* suggest the development of a new rule set for plant functional types that requires the trade-offs of investing in certain key traits that may play important roles in climate change.

McMahon *et al.* believe that in order to make further progress in the field of climate change modeling there needs to be a greater unification of scientists, globally. They suggest the development of an internet based "repository," allowing instant access to new data on biodiversity from monitoring sites around the globe. Such an access point should go a long way toward advancing the accuracy of current and future models. McMahon *et al.* believe that with greater connectivity between the scientific community, and the interlacing of already established models, there can be a great increase in the quality of climate change modeling.

A Framework for Determining the Effect of Global Climate Change and the Response of Species and Ecosystems

Species around the world will need to adapt, migrate, disperse, or evolve to deal with the current and future climate change. Otherwise, they will go extinct. It is thus important, in the effort to preserve biodiversity, to understand what species or habitat is at risk the most. While there are natural methods and responses in place for species, many are further hindered by the development of human populations. Dawson *et al.* (2011) developed a general framework to help aid in this task. Combining methods and models from around the scientific community, they hoped to create a more comprehensive and deeper understanding of the ability of species, habitats, and ecosystems to adapt to climate change. The authors believe this method will further aid conservation efforts globally, as the framework will allow conservationists to look at the affects of climate change from the individual species to its ecosystem to its biosphere. Dawson *et al.* understand the necessity for a complete and deeper understanding of species interactions with their environment, and just how this will affect future species shifts. The authors' framework will aid in future conservation efforts of species and ecosystems.

Current and future climate change is predicted to heavily impact biodiversity globally. Many studies have now been done on the effects of climate change on local species niches, resulting in alarming rates of displacement and extinctions. However, Dawson *et al.* believe that the data being collected in these studies do not tell the full story. The niche-based model, according to the authors, only highlights the species' exposure to global warming. Changes in biodiversity locally and globally are much more complicated than these models can illustrate. The alarming nature of some niche-based models has caused a knee jerk reaction by policy makers, but the authors warn that designing conservation and restoration policies based on one scientific approach is highly risky. Therefore Dawson *et al.* propose integrating known methods and models, and refocusing on the overall vulnerability to global warming on species, ecosystems, habitats, and communities.

The authors state that in addition to temperature, vulnerability is linked directly to exposure, sensitivity, and adaptive capacity. Using multiple sources of evidence from the scientific community, Dawson *et al.* established a general framework for observing the affects of global warming through these three aspects to create a more complete picture of the effects of global warming. By using current niche-based models, direct observation, paleoecological records, ecophysiological models, experimental manipulations, and population models, a more complete picture can be revealed. The initial findings show that biodiversity loss will not be as great as predicted solely by the niche models.

Direct observations create a basic picture of how species are adapting currently to climate change; it appears that species are increasing their ranges and migrations. This isn't the full story however, as currently we do not have a full understanding of range shifts, and species' response to climate change. It is thus necessary to use other methods in conjunction with observational studies. However, the observation data do give us insight into the sensitivity of species to climate change.

Another important method of determining the effect of global warming on our planet is determining how and if species can adapt (i.e. adaptive capability). The authors suggest that species populations have a high ability to adapt through microevolution and migration, however these are difficult data to record. Therefore the authors use past data from the previous glacial transition 20,000–12,000 years ago. The evidence suggests a great capacity of species to adapt. As the authors point out, during the last glacial transition period there is only one species extinction that is attributed solely to climate change.

Dawson *et al.* believe that by using the data above, as well as many other sources, they have developed a vulnerability framework. Using this framework, a more complete picture of how global climate change is affecting, and will affect species in the future, can be developed. Dawson *et al.* found, using their framework, that many plant species will need to disperse rapidly, but will likely be hindered by human development. They then determined that using the long-distance dispersal conservation method to help plants migrate would be appropriate. This is simply one example of a way to use their model. *Dawson et al.* suggest that there are many uses for their framework, as it can be applied at every level, from an individual species to a whole ecosystem. More importantly, the authors stress that it is important to use the framework at every level, as simply looking at the environment in one way will not be enough to understand the actions we must take to help it. The framework developed by *Dawson et al.* will aid the on going conservation efforts, but most importantly will aid the scientific community in gaining a understanding of the larger climate change picture.

A Model for Future Protection and Restoration of Biodiversity in Warming Tropics

Global climate change will greatly affect the niche habitats of endemic and specialized species in the tropical rain forests. Most primary endemic and specialized species inhabit the coolest regions of a rainforest, putting them at risk of the rising temperatures accompanying global climate change. To protect them it is important to preserve remaining rainforest and to restore lost cooling regions. Shoo *et al.* (2011) developed and tested a new model for determining the overall temperatures of tropical regions using elevation, proximity to coast, foliage extent, and other variables. This model will aid in determining what areas are most in need of protection and restoration. The authors discovered a way to quantify natural mechanisms that regulate temperature, allowing them to create a model that will aid conservation efforts in rain forests globally.

The change in global temperature that is causing global climate change has a major impact on species niches and their surrounding environments. Other studies have already determined that there is a large cost to delaying study of and action in preservation of endangered areas (Hannah *et al.* 2007), and therefore Shoo *et al.* concluded that a quantitative model was needed to target key climate refuges for future conservation in rain forests. By observing the preferred temperature niches of local species and then finding the mean and range of temperatures for the key regions, Shoo *et al.* believed they could prioritize the protection and restoration of tropical refuges to maximize future biodiversity in the wake of climate change. Using key geographic traits of areas (i.e. elevation, latitude, distance to stream, distance to coast, foliage cover, clear-sky radiation, cloud off-set, and wind exposure) Shoo *et al.* were able to generate detailed predictions over large spatial scales of temperature variations in the desired region. Shoo *et al.* ran a trial of this quantitative model on the tropical northeastern Australian rainforest.

They began by measuring local temperature ranges using 12 permanent open-air weather stations, which recorded the 24 hour maximum, and minimum temperatures and 23 weather stations deployed by their team, which recorded the temperature in 15-minute intervals from January 2007 to the end of December 2008. Using independent predictor models, the authors developed a model of spatial surfaces for the region, modeling elevation, latitude, distance to stream, distance to coast, foliage cover, clear-sky radiation, cloud off-set, and wind exposure. Then using a linear regression approach for each independent month of recorded data, they developed three equations. The first equation was a base set of predictor variables which included elevation, latitude, distance to stream, distance to coast, foliage cover, clear-sky radiation. The second added on cloud offset, and the third added wind exposure instead of cloud offset. The two extensions to the base model were developed because the authors wanted to see if cloud offset or wind exposure affected the overall data in a significant way, but neither did.

The results of their work showed the utility of a quantitative model to determine future restoration and protection sights for vital cool tropical areas. The three largest determining factors of maximum temperature were elevation, distance to coast, and foliage cover. It is the foliage cover of the rainforest that is the main focus for future conservation efforts. With the model the authors found that in the 8738 km^2 of rainforest the average temperature is 27.55°C with a range of 17.32°C to 35.01°C. Shoo *et al* discovered that 30% of the vertebrates (n=152) in the area live in the first temperature quartile

(<25.88°C) and 39% in the second temperature quartile, both with cooler temperatures than for the rest of the vertebrates studied. The vertebrates in the lowest temperature quartile were also the most specialized, and therefore most in danger of climate and temperature shifts. The 62 endemic vertebrates species studied were broken down to 45%, 39%, 16% and 0% for the first, second, third, and forth quartiles respectively, further showing the need for cooler temperature in the region. The first quartile alone covers 2109 km^2 of the rainforest, and 85% of this is already considered protected area. Another 26% of the rainforest has been cleared or degraded since pre-European settlement. To discover the importance of this lost 26% of the rainforest played had in the regions' temperature, Shoo *et al.* modeled the "precleared" temperatures. The average temperature was 29.45°C with a range of 22.55°C to 33.70°C. The team estimated that about 139 km^2 of the lost forest was once habitat for the lowest temperature quartile of vertebrate. This leaves a total of 189 km^2 of unprotected land, including unprotected land and cleared land.

The rainforest of northeast Australia is a poor model for conservation work because so much of the deforestation has avoided the cooler, more vital regions of the rainforest. But Shoo *et al.* clearly demonstrate the success of this model's ability to be a guide for protection and restoration of tropical regions in an effort to preserve biodiversity. Shoo *et al.* estimate that if 80% of the "precleared" land were restored to its rainforest state that it would dramatically help lower temperatures in that region, aiding nearly half of the species that are home in the coolest regions of rainforest. What is most important about this study is the development of a model that can successfully guide future preservation and restoration projects around the world. In areas of Africa, South America, and Latin America where tropical regions are in danger of human development, the model could prove to be very helpful to determine what areas to protect and restore. The authors helped to reiterate the importance of cool temperature for the diverse, specialized, endemic species in rain forests, and presented a model to aid in their protection. As the world faces further climate change due to human activity this developed model could aid the protection and restoration of biodiversity in tropical regions around the world.

The Amazon's Growth into the Richest Area of Organisms in the World

The Amazon rainforest and the Amazon River support an abundant forest full of biodiversity. Yet, it is still a mystery as to how this region became so rich as it is today. Hoorn *et al.* (2010) pull together resources from around the scientific community to piece together the history of Amazonia. Their research focuses on the effect the development of the Andes had on the entire Amazonian region. The Andes changed its climate, redirected the water flow, distributed soil and nutrients, and brought a great influx of diverse species from North America down to the Amazon. Over a hundred million years the Amazon rainforest slowly developed into what it is today, but there are still many questions on how exactly this happened. Hoorn *et al.* attempt to answer some of these questions, while also raising more. What becomes clear is that the development of a large ecosystem, such as Amazonia, is not a simple process, but rather a long, complicated process dependent on many factors.

Protecting the Amazonian region of South America is critical in preserving regional and global biodiversity. The Amazon rainforest is home to what may be the most diverse and unique terrestrial species. The authors believe that the uplift of the developing Andes largely influenced the ecological development of the Amazonian region, and examine this thesis using a variety of new models and data in the fields of geology, paleontology, ecology, and molecular phylogenies.

In order to understand the effect the growth of the Andes had on the Amazonian rainforest, Hoorn *et al.* first studied the pre-Andean Amazonian region from 10 million years ago (MYA) to 135

MYA. Over the course of continental breakup (135 to 100 MYA) the Amazonian region developed the initial basins that would become home to the modern rainforest, as well as the beginnings of the mouth of the Amazon River. The tectonic plate shifts during this time also began the initial formations of the Andes Mountains. This entire region is known as pan-Amazonia, which existed up to 10 MYA, and extended past the present area of the Amazon into Orinoco, Magdalena, and sometimes into the northern Paraná region. Over the next few million years, pan-Amazonia became home to a variety of mammalian species, freshwater fish species, and even at some points saltwater fish species.

Sixty-five to 34 MYA the movement of tectonic plates southward began creation of the Central Andes, and then about 23 MYA additional plate movement began the creation of the Northern Andes. This development also saw the first of modern plant and animal mountainous species rise in this region. About 12 MYA the region underwent its most intense mountain building. During this period the gap between South America and Panama was closed, giving way to the Great American Biotic Interchange. This brought a great number of new species to the Amazonian region from North America, furthering the diversity that was already taking place. During this time the land continued to advance, as mountains began to surpass 2000 meters in height and basins grew out of the mountainous regions. These changes in geological environment caused rainfall to increase in the southeast. The continued uplift and increased rainfall resulted in erosion and sediment dispersal. Over the next millions of years the sediments made their way westward.

The development of the mountainous regions coincided with the development of a large wetland. The wetland, along with warmer temperatures, brought the rise of many large invertebrates, now extinct. Evidence of seasonal monsoons also gives evidence of a rapidly developing environment, as a water influx becomes a seasonal norm. Around this time there is also evidence of a rise of salinity, giving way to more marine species inland. The overall influence of these marine conditions on Amazonia is still in debate, however. The continued growth of the mountains resulted in the creation of valleys and advanced water systems. Around 10 MYA when the sea level dropped, the Amazon River became fully established by reaching the Atlantic Ocean. This also coincided with the change of the Western Amazon basin from a megawetland to more river conditions, as seen today. This change brought the end for many endemic species, and the rise of grasslands that would later give rise to the forests of today. In the last 3.5 million years the Andes have continued to rise, readjusting river patterns, and fully closing the gap between South America and Panama. The influx of North American plant and animal species, as well as African plant species played large roles in diversifying the Amazonian region during this time, creating the forest and animal species we know today.

What these results mean for the current and future Amazonian region is still unclear, as further specific studies need to be done. However, Hoorn *et al.* show that tree diversity is dependent on wetter, less seasonal areas, and that animal diversity is affected by many factors that need further studying. The younger, western region of Amazonia is home to more species than the older, eastern half. This raises many questions over how diversification occurs, and what drives it. What these data do suggest is that wetter, less seasonal western Amazonia might play a key role in sustaining climates faced with change, while sustaining, and perhaps driving, diversity. What is clear is that there is no simple answer to how Amazonia became so diverse and abundant. There is no one large event in global history that single-handily affected the region, but rather it has been a mix of many events from the formation of the continents onwards.

The Need for More Research and More Conservation in Tropical Biodiversity

Tropical rain forests are home to most of Earth's biodiversity. It is therefore paramount to understand the potential impacts human disturbances in the tropics have on biodiversity. Gibson *et al.* (2011) combine 138 studies to create a global meta-analysis on the impact of human disturbances on tropical biodiversity. The effect of humans differs throughout the world, but is present everywhere. Southeast Asian taxa show the largest sensitivity to human development, while birds are the hardest hit taxonomic group. However, not all species are negatively affected. Some mammals, specifically small mammals, benefited from human disturbances, and all mammals had a considerably lower sensitivity than birds. The resounding findings in this paper are the desperate need for more research to be done, especially in African tropics, as well as the need for conservation of primary forests. Secondary forests were potential habitats for biodiversity conservation, but this paper shows that secondary forests have substantially lower amounts of biodiversity than primary forests. Gibson *et al.* produce the first meta-analysis of biodiversity in the tropics, and reveal the great need for conservation efforts and for more research.

The preservation of primary tropical forests is key to the sustainability of biodiversity, and the dramatic increase of human development in tropical forests could have a huge impact on biodiversity. As more studies are done on the effects on biodiversity from forest degradation, we might be able to find some answers as to how to stop them. Current literature shows varied results depending on the type of impacts studied, most often reporting studies of a specific response in a specific region. Gibson *et al.* attempt to piece together the puzzle of biodiversity in the tropics by analyzing 138 studies. Their goal to deliver a better overall understanding of what is causing biodiversity to change and how it is changing.

The 138 studies that were used in this study span the globe, with a focus on Central America and Southeast Asia. It is therefore important to keep in mind that the current data may be biased toward these two locations. The authors have discovered a huge gap in studies done in Africa, Central America, and India. There is a great need for more research in these areas, especially Africa since it is home to the second largest tropical forest.

The authors used the data presented in the papers to create a metric for understanding the effect of biodiversity. Putting together the specific effects on biodiversity, they developed a standard method for understanding each paper's specific results, allowing them to compare each of the results by region, taxonomic group, metric, and disturbance type.

Even with this hole in the current data, the data on record reveal much. Southeast Asia, the focus of the Asian studies, is home to the most sensitive biota. The authors developed a metric of sensitivity by finding the median effect size, which was 0.51. Any numbers below zero reflected a benefit from the effects of human interference. The studies done in Southeast Asia reveal that there is an effect size of 0.95, which is much higher than any of the other regions studied. The authors suggest that this can be explained by the large increase in human development due to expansion of oil palm monoculture. Africa and South America showed effect sizes of about .35 and .42, respectively, while Central America showed an effect size of about 0.1. The stark difference between Asia, specifically Southeast Asia, and the rest of the regions demonstrates the urgent need for preventative measures against the adverse effects of human development.

Among taxonomic groups there was little difference between arthropods, birds, and plants. Each had an effect size of about 0.6 to 0.7. Mammals, however, showed an effect size of −12, suggesting that some mammals substaintally benefitted from some human disturbances. The authors suggest that this is due to the higher abundance of small mammals in degraded forests, perhaps be because small mammals tend to have a high tolerance to disturbance. Birds showed the most vulnerability of the four taxa, however here it is important to look at what disturbance type affected each taxonomic group most.

Birds were most sensitive to development of agricultural land, while plants are most sensitive to burned or shaded forests. Of the twelve-disturbance types, agricultural land use and abandonment had the largest impacts. The agroforestry and plantations (shaded and un-shaded) were considerably lower, which is to be expected. The lowest effect was found in selective logging, however the value was still positive at 0.11. This finding is supported by other studies, which have found selective logging to preserve large numbers of local species. These findings suggest that selective logging is the best solution to preserve biodiversity. There is however still a large danger in logging. Logging and the long-term effects of logging roads through the forest have the potential to injure primary forests, increase risk of species extinction over the long-term, and further exacerbate already existing issues. So, these seemingly positive results should still be taken with a grain of salt.

Next the authors split the various measures of biodiversity into five response metrics: abundance, community structure and function, demographics, forest structure, and richness. The most common of these metrics are abundance and richness, used in over 75% of the papers surveyed. Richness and forest structure are the most sensitive to human disturbance, with effect sizes of 0.83 and 0.7, respectively. Community structure and function was the next largest impacted, while abundance came next at 0.19. Demographics showed little effect at all. The high level of richness was deemed conservative by the authors because it considered forest specialists and generalists equally. If only specialists were considered richness would be 1.16. The authors, therefore, deem that species richness is a good measure of forest value, and how urgently conservation acts are needed.

The need for more research is perhaps the most important finding of this study, especially in Africa. The other finding of great importance is that secondary forests are of little use in preserving biodiversity. It was believed that secondary forests may be a potential source of biodiversity habitat, but the authors have found secondary forests have significantly lower levels of biodiversity than do primary forests. The conservation of primary forests appear to be the only solution in our effort to preserve biodiversity.

Genetically Modified Crops Benefit Biodiversity and Human Sustainability

The use of genetically modified crops in commercial agriculture has been in debate for many years now, and there exists a worry of how these crops may adversely affect humans, as well as other species. Carpenter (2011) reviews journal articles related to the effect of genetically modified crops on biodiversity, focusing the review on crop diversity, effect on non-target soil organisms, effect on target pests, changes in farming practices, weed diversity, use of pesticides and herbicides, and several other topics. The overall findings of Carpenter are that genetically modified crops have near negligible effects on non-targeted species, while being successful at reducing targeted species populations. There is also evidence that genetically modified crops are already aiding biodiversity by increasing farming yields, reducing the amount of land needed to convert from natural habitat to agricultural land. The increased yields, due to successful reduction of pests, has also resulted in more beneficial farming practices, including more conservative tillage practices and decreases in pesticide and herbicide use. The introduction of genetically modified crops has the potential to be extremely beneficial to both humans and our efforts in preserving biodiversity.

High crop yields are essential as the human population continues to grow. Genetically modified (GM) crops offer an opportunity to increase our crop yields, but what effect do genetically modified crops have on the surrounding environment? Carpenter reviewed research papers and review articles on the effect GM crops have on crop diversity, non-target soil organisms diversity, weed diversity, land use, target organisms, non-target above ground invertebrates, birds, tillage practices, and pesticide use. Using this framework Carpenter was able to outline the potential effect of introducing GM crops on biodiversity. From the beginning it is clear that the largest threat to biodiversity is the conversion of natural habitats into agricultural land. Reviewing the impact of GM crops will give us a better sense if the benefits of GM crops outweigh the costs.

The first issue at hand is changes in crop diversity. Over the history of commercial agriculture our crops have become less diverse as we seek to improve the economic efficiency of their production. This has the potential to put strain on our crops' genetic resources, potentially lowering yield, pest resistance, and quality. The use of GM crops could be a source of re-diversifying our crop selection. The GM genetic strains might mix with wild strains, creating more diversity. It might also be the case that with GM crops lesser used, and previously less cost efficient crops, will be revitalized due to the development their GM varieties; sweet potato is one such example.

The quality of the soil is regulated not as much by what fertilizers we add, as by the organisms that live in it. Fungi and invertebrate species play key roles in sustaining arable soil, and therefore it is important to understand the effect GM crops might have on them. Carpenter used a review of 70 journal articles, which stated there was little to no impact on soil organisms due to the introduction of GM crops. There have been reports that GM crops adversely affect microbial communities, but most of the effect is thought to be due to differences in geography, temperature, plant variety, and soil type. Papers published after this review reached similar conclusions of little to no effect on soil organisms by GM crops. One of the few documented adverse effects was that long exposure to GM corn as the only food source, reduced the growth of snails. From these articles it is clear that GM crops have little impact on soil organisms, and what impact might exist might be due to regional abiotic differences.

The presence of weeds in farming communities has a large impact on local biodiversity. The more weeds present in an area the more herbicide needed, and more weeds will result in changes of tillage practices. In reviewing journal articles, Carpenter has found that the introduction of GM crops has resulted in declines of weed populations. In the U.S., a survey in six states found that farmers report a 36 to 70% decline in weed pressure. A study done in the U.K. found that introduction of GM sugar, beet, and oilseed rape resulted in declines of weeds and weed seed, but GM corn resulted in increased weed numbers. This resistance in corn fields is most likely due to the development of new strains of glyphosate resistant (GR) weeds, but however there are few reports of such weeds found globally.

As mentioned earlier, the most direct adverse effect on biodiversity is the conversion of natural land to agricultural land, so Carpenter's results show GM crops are more productive and require less land. Carpeter shows that GM crops increase crop yields from 0 to 7% in developed countries and 16 to 30% in developing countries. Thus, GM crops have the potential to save biodiversity by allowing farmers to avoid converting natural lands.

Perhaps one of the more important direct aspects of use of GM crops is their effect on targeted pest species. Papers from around the globe unanimously show that GM crops decrease the levels of pest populations. Studies in China, California, Arizona, Mississippi, and Maryland all show declines in their respective pest populations over time. This has a very positive impact on other species biodiversity as the increase in pest control results in decreased use of pesticide.

The effect of GM crops on above ground invertebrates has been found to be negligible. Over 360 journal articles were reviewed that covered this topic, and they almost all support the use of GM crops when compared to their effects against non-target invertebrates. Papers that did find that beneficial species were declining due to the introduction of GM crops due to inadvertent poisoning through multitrophic exposure lose of prey, or reduction in prey quality, stated that these effects were nothing compared to the effect that physical agriculture practices had on these species.

The effect on birds was counter to theory; the decreased levels of invertebrates and weeds due to the introduction of GM crops was thought to decrease bird population levels, however crops of GM sugar beet and maize were found to have increased bird populations. This may be due, however, to local changes in bird populations outside of the introduction of GM crops.

Another very important change in agricultural practices due to the introduction of GM crops is the change in tillage practices. With the introduction of the stronger, more resistant GM crops farmers are adopting conservative tillage and no-tillage policies. Tillage disturbs the land, and hastens erosion, as well as releasing herbicides and pesticides beyond the farmland. Introduction of GM crops aid in reducing these adverse effects.

The introduction of GM crops, on a whole, seems to provide many more benefits than not. While there have been cases of GM crops hurting farming production, this has not been the case for most adopters. Carpenter concludes that the use of GM crops will greatly aid our fight to feed our growing population, while supporting our efforts to preserve local biodiversity. Many of the opined adverse effects of GM crops, if they exist, seem to be negligible. Thus, the future of GM crops is positive, especially as new technologies continue to be developed. The use of GM crops in commercial agriculture may go a long way to aiding efforts to preserve natural habitats.

No Correlation Between Yield Production and Biodiversity in Large-Scale Farming

There is a growing concern about the amount of food being produced and the growth of the human population. In an effort to meet the demands of population growth it is feared that many natural habitats will have to be replaced by agricultural land. This would be hugely detrimental to biodiversity, especially in tropical regions, which are home to most of the world's biodiversity and 13% of human agriculture. Although more wildlife-friendly agriculture practices have been put forward, they are rarely used on a large scale because it is believed they decrease the total yield. Clough et al. (2011) explore this argument in Indonesian cocoa agroforestry plantations. They discovered that there is no correlation between biodiversity and agricultural yield, opening up many possibilities in large-scale wildlife friendly agricultural practices. They also explored possible ways to benefit yield and biodiversity in trees and birds, giving an example for a new way of thinking about farming and biodiversity conservation. While their findings do not suggest that wildlife friendly farming practices will end the depletion in biodiversity, as primary forests still are home to many more species than any other area on earth, it is a step forward as we attempt to feed our growing population and conserve the planet and the other species on it.

The importance of food and agriculture in our culture is unquestionable, and the global importance of agriculture will continue to grow in the years to come. As human populations grow there is an increasing demand for food. Agriculture, however, is one of the main threats to global biodiversity. As farms try to increase yields to meet increasing demands, removing natural habitats and increasing farmland is often the action taken. If wild species are to survive then a balance must be found between agriculture and biodiversity. There is the potential for biodiversity-friendly farming. This farming method is often criticized for decreasing the yield quantity because of the focus on biodiversity preservation. Clough et al. explore this argument in Indonesian cacao farms. The argument that wildlife friendly farming practices is ineffective on larger scales is put to the test. The authors evaluated the possibility of combining high species diversity and high yields and where this might be done.

The authors chose to focus on tropical regions in Indonesia because of the high biodiversity combined with the high human populations density. Furthermore, agriculture in tropic regions compasses 13% of the total agricultural system globally, and thus is an important area for future agricultural output.

Clough *et al.* broke the study into two parts: a field study and a survey study. The field study consisted of data collected on yield and species richness in nine different taxonomic groups, during a two-year period. The authors used the land of 43 smallholder cacao agroforestry system in Sulawesi, Indonesia. Only mature plots ten to twenty years old were chosen for the study. Also, the authors studied the possible relationship between biodiversity and yield as distance to a natural forest changed.

The survey portion of the study focused on 60 cacao plantations that were run only by the owners, and were not affected by the study. Only tree species were used as a measurement of biodiversity, however other agronomic data were recorded. These data were used mostly for a better understanding of general yield patterns throughout the regions.

The authors discovered a surprising result once their data were collected, there was little to no correlation between species richness and yield. This general lack of correlation could potentially have large impacts on farming methods, but first the authors explored what does affect species richness and yield.

They found that differences in region and altitude had large impacts on species richness, but it was mainly associated with distance from forests and shade by trees. There was a clear negative relationship between distance from forest and species richness. Plots with high levels of trees and shade had more bird species, but had fewer light-dependent species, such as herbs and butterflies.

Yield was mainly negatively affected by the amount of shade a plot received, however distance to forest had a small positive effect. Other variables proved to have little effect on yield. Through the survey portion of the study, it was determined that labor and pesticide use were the largest determinants of yield.

In an attempt to find a possible method of sustaining high yields and high biodiversity the authors focused on the effects of trees, yield, and birds. They found that birds were more dependent on tree height than total amount of shade, whereas yield was affected by shade. Therefore it may be possible to increase bird habitat with taller, but fewer trees, resulting in less shade.

This study reveals that it is possible to have wildlife friendly farms that produce high yields. These findings suggest that wildlife friendly policies can be, and should be, implemented in agriculture without fear of yield loss. The authors also caution that their findings may be inaccurate because there may be a lag in time between the presence of farms and their effect on biodiversity. This is why the authors chose the most established and mature agroforestry sites. More data need to be collected to continue to record the effects on the practices of wildlife friendly agricultural on biodiversity and yield. At first glance, though, the findings of Clough *et al.* are quite stunning and exciting, leaving the potential for new wildlife friendly farming practices that produce high yields for a growing human population.

Conclusions

The scientific community is just beginning to compile much of the data on biodiversity that has been collected over the past few decades, and we are starting to see a clearer picture. Our impact on biodiversity is undeniable, and certainly worrying, however, there certainly are opportunities to minimize it with better agricultural methods. As the methods for collecting and calculating biodiversity improve, and as more data in data poor regions become available, a clearer picture will be created on our effect on global species biodiversity. Until then it would be best to begin preserving the richest areas of life, namely primary tropical forests, learning new methods for combining preservation and agriculture and lumbering and society.

The risk of biodiversity loss is too high for us to sit idly when we know we are capable doing something about it.

References Cited

Carpenter, J.E. 2011. Impacts of GM crops on biodiversity. Landes Bioscience 2:1, 1–17.

Clough, Y., Barkmann, J., Juhrbandt, J., Kessler, M., Wanger, T.C., Anshary, A., Buchori, D., Cicuzza, D., Darras, K., Putra, D.D., Erasmi., S., Pitopang, R., Schmidt, C., Schulze, C.H., Seidel, D., Steffan-Dewenter, I., Stenchly, K., Vidal, S., Weist, M., Wielgoss, A.C., Tscharntke, T. 2011. Combining high biodiversity with high yields in tropical agroforests. PNAS 108:20, 8311–8316.

Dawson, T.P., Jackson, S.T., House, J.I., Prentice, I.C., Mace, G.M., 2011. Beyond predictions: biodiversity conservation in a changing climate. Science 332, 53–58.

Gibson L., Lee T.M., Koh L.P., Brook B.W., Gardner T.A., Barlow J., Peres C.A., Bradshaw C.J.A., Laurance W.F., Lovejoy T.E. 2011. Primary forests are irreplaceable for sustaining tropical biodiversity. Nature 478, 378–381.

Hoorn, C., Wesselingh, F.P., ter Steege, H., Bermudez, M.A., Mora, A., Sevink, J., Sanmartín, I., Sanchez-Meseguer, A., Anderson, C.L., Figueiredo, J.P., Jaramillo, C., Riff, D., Negri, F.P., Hooghiemstra, H., Lundberg, J., Stadler, T., Särkinen, T., Antoneli, A., 2010. Amazonia Through Time: Andean Uplift, Climate Change, Landscape Evolution, and Biodiversity. Science 330, 927–931.

Maclean, I. and Wilson R. 2011. Recent ecological responses to climate change support   predictions of high extinction risk. PNAS Early Edition: 1–6.

McMahon, S., Harrison, S., Armbruster, S.W., Bartlein, P., Beale, C., Edwards, M., Kattge, J., Midgley G., Morin, X., Prentice I.C., 2011. Improving assessment and modelling of climate change impacts on global terrestrial biodiversity. Trends in Ecology and Evolution 26, 249–259.

Shoo, L. P., Storlie, C., Vanderwal, J., Little, J. and Williams, S. E., 2011. Targeted protection and restoration to conserve tropical biodiversity in a warming world. Global Change Biology 17, 186–193.

5. Global Effects of Climate Change on Wildfire: Causal Relationships of Fire, the Natural Environment, and Human Activities

Lindon Pronto

Climate change and human activity is significantly impacting the frequency and severity of wildfires across the globe. Although climate change and human population are the overarching factors affecting wildfires in the current dialogue, the issues are more complex and often not fully understood. These issues range from global temperature increases and severe drought cycles to the relatively new phenomenon of the wildland urban interface (WUI). This is the area where structures are integrated with or immediately surrounded by areas of moderate to high fire risk and are directly linked to fuel types and topographic features. Because climate change is such a highly politicized issue, there are generally limited governmental frameworks that enact policies that encourage a deeper understanding of the causal relationships between climate issues and population impacts on wildfire. While politicians debate whether climate change exists, scientists are showing us that it is producing real threats; some of these threats are the loss of life and property as a result of wildfire, as well as the critical economic impacts of suppressing these evermore frequently occurring, catastrophic fires.

Knowing exactly when fire regimes have changed over history and on a global scale is difficult, but there are some studies that have provided this information for specific geographic areas. Wathen (2011) reports one possible explanation for current fire regimes in the Sierra Nevada is the evidence of climate teleconnections over the past 1,800 years between the Sierra's and Greenland that suggested abruptly changing climate features. During that time period the onset of severe droughts in Nevada coincided with severe fires and erosion in Northern California. Wathen implies that some of these abrupt climate changes during the late Holocene are responsible for causing some mountain slopes to have vegetation types that were out of equilibrium to the climate conditions, subsequently leading to an increase in wildfire frequency and severity over time (Wathen). In more recent history, Dimitrakopoulos *et al.* (2011) concluded that there was a significant threshold change in Greece during the late 1970s during which more severe summer and annual drought cycles coupled with urbanization and higher rates of arson, led to spike in fire frequency and total annual area burned. Even so, perhaps one of the most recent areas to be added to the list of climate-induced fire regime changes was illuminated by Mack *et al.* (2011), in a revealing study about wildfire in the Arctic Tundra biome. As global temperatures rise, changing climatic conditions have introduced wildfire-induced carbon (C) releases in the Arctic tundra that have not been observed in many millennia. They found that these tundra fires have the potential to significantly amplify global warming through the release of concentrated C pools into the atmosphere—pools that in some cases are thousands of years old.

Recent science is showing us that climate change is the umbrella for shifting fire regimes around the globe. In Australia, fire intervals have historically been influenced by spatial variation in vegetation and landscape connectivity. Though areas of Australia differ from other landscapes, the effects of climate change may soon override these traditional fire regime norms that have been reliant on topographical features and vegetation connectivity (O'Donnell *et al.* 2011). In Portugal, fire activity has increased significantly while being exacerbated by fuel type, slope and elevation, and notably, proximity to roads and populated areas as well (Marques *et al.* 2011). In Alaska, rising global temperatures have caused seasonal changes in various ways particularly acute at higher latitudes. The summer of 2004 was the most severe fire season on record, largely attributed to a severe weather event, for which they determined climate change as being an underlying factor (Wendler *et al.* 2010).

The effects of climate change on fire can be further broken down to look at short and long term effects of fires on carbon stocks, or even how disease outbreaks have the potential to amplify fire severity such as Sudden Oak Death on the California coast (Metz *et al.* 2011). As forests contain the planet's largest terrestrial carbon stocks, wildfires, by burning forests, release a significant amount of this stored carbon into the atmosphere extremely rapidly. This release interrupts a longer cycle where carbon is sequestered by growing trees and then is finally rereleased during the decomposition of the vegetation. North and Hurteau (2011) expose how forest management practices can lessen the effects of wildfires on tree mortality and affect higher survivability during dangerous fires in Northern California.

Future models and predictions only point towards the development of further significant climatic conditions that are conducive of more frequent and extreme wildfires. In Brazil, based on future climate models concerning the Potential Fire Index (PFI), changes in vegetation composition are expected to greatly increase the magnitude of the PFI. Furthermore, climate conditions are expected to potentially extend the fire seasons as a result of longer drought periods especially in the Amazonia (Justino *et al.* 2010). Similarly in China, according to future models, fire danger, fire activity, area burned, and fire season duration are all expected to increase significantly over the next century. Xiao-rui *et al.* (2011) concluded that the above phenomena would in fact occur under two of four climate change scenarios outlined by the Intergovernmental Panel on Climate Change (IPCC) covering the period from 1991–2100.

Perhaps the issue that raises the most public concern and political dialogue is the issue of public safety, loss of property, and the costs of suppressing fires. This collection of papers hardly makes a dent in these important issues because it is the subject worthy of many volumes; this is due to the plethora of geographic technicalities such as climate and fuel type, accessibility, proximity to population, economies of scale and resource allocation, skill level and suppression resources available, technology…and the list goes on. Included are two papers that do focus less on field work or climate models. First is a paper by Cova *et al.* (2011) which maps some of the dangers of increased wildfire prospects up against the ever and rapidly expanding wildland urban interface (WUI). The threat analyzed here is the limited access routes, which make immediate egress in the event of a severe wildfire threat, an additional hazard for these communities. Finally, is a paper that deals with solutions for a forest management plan that takes small communities located deep within the WUI into account as they are often left out of the equation for reasons largely to do with economies of scale. This approach works to combine forest management, energy acquisition, sustainable design, and community participation to address not just the threat of wildfires, but the rest of the challenges that face these types of communities (Yablecki *et al.* 2011). These last two examples are immediate issues of public safety and strong constructive suggestions for future policy building and regulatory foresight for population expansion into fire-prone areas.

*   *   *

Following in the footsteps of my father, at the age of 17, I completed my basic training as a wildland firefighter. In the following summer of 2007 I reported to my duty station as a newly hired "professional" federal firefighter in the USDA Forest Service in northern California. My lifelong relationship to fire might have begun when I tripped and fell in one as small child, but it certainly has developed over many years of fuel treatment and fire prevention projects on my family's property, through countless dinner conversations, and eventually it led to me dedicating a significant part of my life to protecting forests and communities and combating fires. Since, I have had the opportunity to fight fires in six states and have the pleasure of sharing a common passion with my father, with the ability to tap into his over 30 years of experience. It has fascinated me to open my eyes to the global phenomenon of wildfire and climatology, deviating away from my narrowed understanding centered on fire characteristics and fire management practices in the western United States. It was exciting for me to read studies about fires I fought, augmenting my memories of adrenaline and gritty backbreaking labor, with the scientific effects of immediate carbon release in the atmosphere, or the subsequent effects of ash on stream ecosystems.

In this selection of articles I have attempted to first show the effects of climate conditions on wildfires from past examples to future daunting models of predicted wildfire potential. This general scientific foundation is intended to convey the broader sense of increasing wildfire frequency and severity as it is rooted in changing climatic conditions shown on a larger geographic scale. Secondly, I chose some studies to focus more on specific issues within this dialogue such as carbon stock release or the effect of disease on fire severity. Finally I wanted to end with two papers that begin to address the dangers of population centers within the WUI as well as looking at a multifaceted solutions based approach to addressing fire, fuels management, energy acquisition, and carbon emissions as a cluster issue. My overall goal was to represent the issue on a global scale, though admittedly the majority of the focus is placed on North America as there was a higher availability in studies in the United States and Canada. Had I had more time, I would have also liked to include more studies from South America, parts of Africa and especially Australia and Russia—where wildfire events have been particularly cata-strophic in recent years.

Impact of Drought on Wildland Fires in Greece: Implications of Climate Change?

A spike in wildfire frequency and amount of area burned in the past decades has been increasingly attributed to factors induced by climate change. Though shifting wildfire regimes are strongly af-fected by more direct human actions, such as increased rates of arson or the effects of urbanization on rural land use, a study by Dimitrakopoulos et al. (2011), chose to focus on the impacts of drought on wildfire activity in the country of Greece. The study ana-lyzed data from weather stations representing all of Greece over the 37 year period between 1961 and 1997. This time period was chosen because it presented the greatest uninterrupted time interval in the available data. The study sought to prove that an increase in severity of annual and summer droughts has resulted in higher rates of wild-fires and the total area burned. The study concluded that there was a statistically significant increase in fire activity and a positive correla-tion between it and annual drought episodes. It also showed that fire activity has increased significantly since 1978, and that drought played a larger role on fire activity in the more humid and cooler re-gions of Greece.

The area studied groups together 17 prefectures into five geo-graphic regions denoted as Northern, Western, Central, Eastern, and Southern Greece. The prefectures used in the study were chosen for the availability of 37 years of data from official meteorological sta-tions. This study represented drought by the Standard Precipitation Index (SPI) and measured the two main phenomena of annual drought (expressed as SPI12) and summer drought (expressed as SPI6). The study identified all prefectures under respective climate types based on precipitation levels and were expressed as "semi-dry, semi-wet, and wet." Wildfire activity, characterized by number of fires and area burned, was also tracked in all 17 prefectures. Aside from applying SPI values to the entire 37 year period, the study was broken down into two separate sub-periods of 1961–1977 and 1978–1997 for data analysis purposes. Dimitrakopoulos et al. were able to detect several fire regime shifts using the extant data with Change Point Analyzing software; by observing the shifts, the data allowed them to determine that a threshold change occurred in 1977. This was significant for analyzing all data during the second sub-period from 1978 to 1997.

The results confirmed the trend that wildfires had increased steadily from 1961 to 1997 in all areas of Greece. More specifically the Northern, Southern and Western areas exhibited a stronger more significant change than the other two regions. Moreover, there was a significantly higher level of fire activity in the second sub-period, as well as a notable increase in area burned for that period as compared to the earlier sub-period pre 1978. Interestingly, the increased rate of fire occurrences between all the regions was not consistent with the area burned geographically, which depended on the region (climate).

By following the SPI12 and SPI6 values, it was determined that both annual and summer drought episodes increased significantly after 1977 for both the Northern and Western regions. Excluding Eastern Greece, all other areas showed a strong positive correlation between fire occurrence and drought episodes during the entire 37 year period. More specifically, Southern and Central Greece (historically exhibiting the highest level of fire activity) did not correlate with the SPI12 value, indicating that it was most heavily influenced by summer droughts (SPI6) alone. While the different regions correlated with both one another and with summer and annual droughts in different ways, the overall effect was that an increase in starts (new fires) geographically mirrored the greater area burned in the cooler more humid climates when more frequent droughts were present.

The overall trends show that between 1961 and 1997, the mean area burned almost quadrupled in Northern Greece nearly tripling in the other districts, while the number of fires almost doubled in Northern and Western Greece. These implications for a global climate change are echoed by increased fire activity in other parts of Europe as well as the rest of the world. In this study, it is apparent that in Central and Southern Greece (warmer and drier) drought episodes during the summer were most detrimental to fire activity while the other regions exhibited increased fire activity when the annual precipitation levels fell, inducing increased fire behavior in response to lower fuel moistures etc.

One interesting contradiction in the results displayed that between the two sub-periods, drought and fire occurrence correlated more significantly leading up to 1978, while a stronger correlation occurred between drought and area burned in the second sub-period after 1977. Dimitrakopoulos et al. offer the following explanation for why this is so: The contradiction lies in the actual cause of individual fires. During the 1961–1977 period, rural Greece was much more heavily populated and the most common cause of fires was negligence. By the late 1970s, urbanization redistributed the population, effecting rural land use, and apparently resulting in a dramatic increase in arson cases. Furthermore, the common denominator for large fires besides high temperature and low Dead Fuel Moisture Content is wind; arson fires can account for large area burned due to their timing with wind.

In conclusion, during the 37 year period, there was a positive correlation with increase of fire activity and annual drought episodes. In Northern and Western Greece alone, fire activity was influenced by both annual and summer drought episodes (which increased after 1977) as opposed to only the summer ones. A possible result of climate change marked a period of prolonged drought in Greece after 1977, which consequently matches a significant increase in the number of fires and area burned during the second period. Overall, the first sub-period 1961–1977 was characterized by its number of fire occurrences to drought correlation, whereas the second sub-period

1978–1997 exhibited a higher correlation to drought and total area burned. Finally, the effects of climate change (increased drought episodes) had a more profound effect on fire activity in wetter colder regions of Greece where historically fire occurrence and area burned was lower. Increased drought episodes have visually impacted wildfire activity in Greece, while current climate change models suggest that further similar trends will, in the future, result in more severe and frequent fires in the Mediterranean region.

Future Impacts of Climate Change on Forest Fire Danger in Northeastern China

As a result of global climate change, many areas around the world will be more prone to increased wildfire activity. Wildfires will become more frequent, burn more intensely, and will burn larger areas; additionally, fire seasons (time periods during which fire is most active) will in many cases be observed for longer durations annually. In a study by Xiao-rui et al. (2011), projections of climate change effects on wildfire danger in the boreal forests of northeastern China were made for the remainder of the century. These future effects were weighed against and validated by historical regional climate data for the baseline period of 1961–1990. The purpose of the study was to prove that fire danger, fire activity, area burned, and fire season duration would all increase significantly over the next century. Xiao-rui et al. concluded that the above phenomena would in fact occur under two of four climate change scenarios outlined by the Intergovernmental Panel on Climate Change (IPCC) covering the period from 1991–2100.

The area chosen for this study encompassed three general areas of boreal forest in northeastern China, accounting for about 37% of the total forested area in the country. These areas were the Daxing'an mountains, the Xiaoxing'an mountains, and the Changbai Mountain forest region. The overall terrain consists of plains in the central area and mountains in the east and west. The study used a validation period of 30 years based on data available from the China Meteorological Data and Sharing Network, where 107 weather stations were located within the study area. Xiao-rui et al. chose to use the Canadian Forest Fire Weather Index (FWI) System to analyze changes to fire danger and the fire season for future periods under IPCC Special Report on Emission Scenarios (SRES) models A2 and B2. The FWI is calculated on the basis of six factors that shape the effect of fuel moisture and wind on fire behavior. The two models used from the IPCC Special Report on Emission Scenarios demonstrate an estimated global average surface temperature warming of 1.4–5.4°C between now and 2100. Both A2 and B2 fall under the "regionalization" scenario (heterogeneous world) where A2 is global temperature increase under a projected approach of regionally orientated economic development, while B2 is a projected approach of localized efforts of environmental sustainability (IPCC, 2007). Additionally projections were made for the overall time periods of a) 2020s, b) 2050s, and c) 2080s; sub-periods examined changes by individual decade. Data sets were illustrated under both A2 and B2 scenarios.

For the study area, two peak times took place during each fire season. First, an approximately three-quarter percent of annual fires occurred during the spring season from March to May, while in the fall period in October, fewer than 10% occurred but accounted for nearly one-quarter of the annual area burned. As a result of these findings, the study was adjusted to account for the two separate fire season peaks under both the A2 and B2 IPCC scenarios. The overall historical trend of the Fire Weather Index (FWI) was high in the spring, and relatively low in autumn; this correlates to future FWI projections, with a notable spike in the 2080s. Geographically, heightened FWI and fire activity were predicted for most of the region especially in the southeast, while few and temporary decreases in high risk fire days were observed. The east-central region exhibited the overall highest FWI values under both models by 2080. Also by

2080, the potential burned areas under scenario A2 are expected to increase by 10% in the spring peak and by 23% in autumn, while under B2 an increase of 18% and 35% respectively, was predicted. One of the more critical effects of global warming is the number of days of fire seasons. This study suggests that for northeastern China, the number of days that exhibit high or extreme fire danger may by 2080 increase by more than 20 days in the Daxing'an Mountains and Xiaoxing'an Mountains, and 41–60 days in the Changbai Mountain region. This trend is expected to be most obvious in the southeast and northwest regions.

The three most important factors that drive fire behavior are fuel, weather, and topography. An important element that was not accounted for in this study is the potential impact of 100 years of climate change on fuel type. The authors of this study suggest that in order to gain a clearer understanding for developing a fire management strategy, it is important that future research focus on incorporating additional effects of long-term climate change on successional vegetation changes in burned areas or areas of temperature induced plant regime shifts. In conclusion, Xiao-rui et al. contend that under the temperature increases outlined by the IPCC models, the threat of wildfires will increase, a greater area will be burned, and certain geographic areas will exhibit significantly lengthened annual periods of high FWI values during the peak spring and autumn fire season. The authors hope that this study can aide in shaping future fire management strategy and practice through knowledge of these future climate scenarios, such as through improving elements like prescribed burning and initial attack-phase fire suppression responses.

Climatology of Alaskan Wildfires with Special Emphasis on the Extreme Year of 2004

As global temperatures rise, the seasons shift in various ways depending on their latitude. For many areas such as Interior Alaska, the annual dry season has become longer and surface fuels have consequently become drier; this has led to an increase of wildfire frequency and severity. Wendler et al. (2010) conducted a 55 year analysis of the various conditions conducive for and associated with, predominantly lightning induced fires in Interior Alaska. With a special emphasis on the extreme year of 2004, the authors examined data for lightning and fire ignition, number of fires versus area burned, and air quality and composition. Special emphasis was placed on the year 2004 where specific fire and climate data, weather, particulate matter, and carbon monoxide concentration, were all examined within the broader context of the whole 55 year data set. They determined that 2004 was the worst fire season on record (in terms of area burned) and that there has been an overall trend in increased wildfire severity and occurrence. Although the unique weather patterns for the summer of 2004 were attributed to the severity of the year, they did show that climate change has been an underlying factor. Furthermore they demonstrated that there were four major fire seasons burning an area greater than 10,000 km² in the last 27 years, as opposed to only two in the previous 28 years.

The authors examined the Palmer Drought Severity Index and the Canadian Drought Code, against both the number of wildfires and the area burned in order to find any significant correlations. Lightning-caused fire data were collected by the Alaska Lightning Detection Network operated by the Bureau of Land Management and the Alaska Fire Service. These data were then used to show the spatial distribution of the lightning strikes, the mean monthly strike count, and the diurnal variation of the strikes. Additionally, temperatures and precipitation patterns were evaluated in terms of lightning activity levels; they found that as temperature increased, so did the lightning activity.

General historical data from 1955–2009 showing number of fires and area burned were retrieved from the Alaska Fire Service, while very detailed data from the 2004 fire season were compiled. On average, 3,775 km² burn annually in Alaska, of which about 90%

occurs within the interior of the state as bounded by the Brooks Range in the north, and the Alaska Range in the south. During the 55 year study period, about 93% of fires were started by an average of 32,000 lightning strikes per year. Statistical analyses showed a correlation coefficient of r=0.67 in the ratio of lightning strikes to resulting wildfires, with an estimate one fire per every 600 strikes. Furthermore this relationship is much higher when positive and negative strikes are evaluated independently of overall fire starts. Positive down-strikes occurring during dry conditions are more infrequent than negative down-strikes which are usually accompanied by precipitation. Despite the lower frequency of positive down-strikes, they are four times more likely to result in a fire. The vast majority of lightning occurs during the months of June and July.

In the summer of 2004, a record 27,200 km² burned (well over 6,700,000 acres), or an area greater than any 6 of the smallest states in the US. It was in this year that many areas around the state set record high temperatures. Additionally, and what is believed responsible for the extremity of the fires in 2004, is the unique weather patterns that occurred. Anticyclonic conditions resulted in unusually clear skies and the third driest summer on record. For calculating the correlation of climate conditions and fire occurrence, the authors found that the Canadian Drought Code (CDC) was more effective than the more commonly used Palmer Drought Severity Index (PDSI). Beginning with below normal snowpack in the spring, a semi-permanent upper-ridge followed with above normal temperatures and below normal rainfall. During two distinct periods of 4 weeks and 3 weeks fires burned an area of 16, 200km² and 8,000km², respectively.

Air quality during this time period deteriorated severely, dramatically reducing visibility and causing significant health risks to the population. Wendler et al. chose to focus on visibility, particulate matter, carbon monoxide (CO) concentration, and radiative fluxes. They found that during the worst of one of the more severe smoke events, visibility was <1/4 mile, fine particle matter exceeded 1,000 μg/m³, while CO concentration levels reached a value of 10.3 ppm; maximum levels prior to smoke never exceeded 1.0 ppm. The transmissivity was calculated as the percent of outside solar radiation that reached the surface as direct solar radiation. During the smoke events, less than 10% of direct radiation occurred. When the CO concentration level and the particulate matter were correlated, there was an overall variance of 72% and 80% during the two major burn periods; they concluded that a relative abundance of CO in relation to particle matter is to be expected for the older smoke of the second period.

Due to the increase in temperature of 1°C in Alaska over the past half century, more frequent and severe wildfire events can be attributed to the latter increase, even when they start nearly exclusively from natural causes as only opposed to increasing human activities in wildland areas. For example, this study shows that during the first half of the study period, 6 years with mean summer temperatures above 16°C occur, while for the second half, this occurred nine times. Similarly, severe fire seasons (>10,000 km² burned) increased from 2 to 4 events from the first 28 years to the second 27 years. Furthermore wildfire events where >5,000 km² burned, increased from three to eight events. This pattern can be contributed to an overall trend of quick or prolonged drying of the surface fuels and soils that increase the likelihood of ignition from a lightning strike. This study synthesizes data to try and recognize conditions for severe fire events and thereby perhaps aide in predicting efforts needed by fire suppression forces in near-future situations; however it does admit that predicting the severity and length of future fires seasons is largely speculative as it can only be based on previous climate patterns of the past 30 years.

Characterization of Wildfires in Portugal

An increase in forest fires in Portugal supports climate change models suggesting that the two phenomena are linked. In recent decades the occurrence of wildfires, their severity, and the area burned, have all increased. In an effort to help in formulating a fire management plan, Marques *et al.* (2011) conducted a study to characterize wildfires in Portugal. The object of the study was to demonstrate trends in fire activity and examine how fuel type, fuel load, elevation, and socioeconomic factors have bearing on fire severity. What the authors found was that fire behaved selectively based on fuel type, slope and elevation, and proximity to roads and populated areas. Furthermore, they established that shrubs displayed the most significant fire activity potential, especially at higher elevations on slopes greater than 5% and further away from socioeconomic influences.

Using historical fire information data, a 33-year-long period from 1975 to 2007 was used as a basis for observing trends in fire occurrence, proximity, and severity. Burned area mapping was established through the use of high-resolution remote sensing data by the Remote Sensing Laboratory of Instituto Superior de Agronomia. The study was broken down into three separate 5 year sub-periods (1987–1991, 1990–1994, and 2000–2004) in an attempt to minimize the effects of land cover changes over time. From land cover maps the authors were able to identify fuel types and distribution. In addition to devising 10 classes of cover types for the purpose of the study, Marques *et al.* identified altitude, slope, proximity to roads, and population density as four additional variables for modeling purposes. Altitude and slope data were obtained from the country's digital terrain model (DTM); GIS overlays from the Instituto Nacional de Estatística provided data on road proximities and population density. Relationships between Ecological and socioeconomic variability and fire occurrences during the three sub-periods were largely based on statistical models.

Over the 33 year period fire perimeter data show that there were 35,194 wildfires which were greater than 5 ha in size. Area burned per year ranged from 15,500 ha in 1977 to 440,000 ha in 2003, where a single fire was responsible for 58,000 ha alone. The first sub-period (1987–1991) had 7,672 starts; the second sub-period (1990–1994) exhibited significantly calmer fire activity with 5,703 starts. The third and final sub-period (2000–2004), was characterized by a significant increase in fire occurrence and size; while the period had 7,383 starts, the area burned was over 43% greater than the first sub-period and 182% for the second sub-period respectively. Most notably the final period exhibited the occurrence of four very large fires being greater than 20,000 ha each in size. There were no fires greater than 20,000 ha during the first 25 years of data.

Weighted generalized linear models (WGLM) proved that the number one high risk fuel was shrubs, followed by mixed stands, softwoods and hardwoods; individual species added variance based on fuel loading, resin, and foliage essential oil content. Marques *et al.* also observed that fires occurred more frequently at higher elevations, which was attributed to higher lightning activity levels (LAL) and escaped pastoral burns. An additional factor found more generally at higher elevations was that of greater slope which contributed to faster rate of spread. In populated areas in Portugal, although human activity is the number one cause of wildfires, their proximity to roads and population centers allows for a very quick response time from firefighters who are often able to extinguish the fires when they are still small. When fires occurred away from populated areas where there was limited or no access, data show that these fires tend to become very large, especially in mountainous areas where slope accelerates rate of spread. There was a positive correlation between distance from populated areas and the area burned.

Through this study, Marques *et al.* were able to characterize wildfire in Portugal with special attention to socioeconomic influences, fuel type, and landscape specific variability. The technique which made this approach possible was the use of weighted generalized linear models which highlighted the relationships of ecological and socioeconomic factors. This study is intended to provide a starting point for policy makers to develop an appropriate and effective fire management plan that is current with wildfire activity trends and congruent with the possible effects of climate change. It provides a context for developing fire prevention practices and policies; furthermore, it suggests continued work in this subject area to translate these results into functioning fire prevention and suppression models for the country of Portugal.

Carbon Loss from an Unprecedented Arctic Tundra Wildfire

As increased frequency and severity of wildfires in historically fire-prone areas pose one set of threats to our ever-more concerning climate situation, scientists have identified a new threat to rising global atmospheric CO_2 levels. Not since the early Holocene epoch has there been any significant wildfire activity or the presence of typical fire regimes within the Arctic tundra biome. As global temperatures rise, changing climatic conditions have introduced wildfire-induced carbon (C) releases in the Arctic tundra that have not been observed in many millennia (perhaps 10,000 years or more). Mack *et al.* (2011) examined the Anaktuvuk River fire that burned 1,039 km² of Arctic tundra on the North Slope of the Brooks Range in Alaska, USA, in 2007; this single fire burned more than double the cumulative area burned in the region over the past half-century. They concluded that the C released from this one fire supports the hypothesis that tundra fires have the potential to significantly amplify global warming through the release of concentrated C pools into the atmosphere that in some cases are thousands of years old.

Mack *et al.* report that the Anaktuvuk River fire burned 1,039 km² removing $2,016 \pm 435 \, g \, C \, m^{-2}$ and $64 \, g \, N \, m^{-2}$ (or about 400 years of N accumulation) from the ecosystem, an amount they say is two orders of magnitude larger than annual net C exchange in undisturbed tundra. Furthermore they report that "the approximately 2.1 teragrams of C [released] into the atmosphere, was an amount similar in magnitude to the annual net C sink for the entire Arctic tundra biome averaged over the last quarter of the twentieth century." Approximately 60% of this C loss was from soil organic matter. Radiocarbon dating of residual soil layers showed the maximum age of soil C that was lost in the fire, was 50 years old.

The study area was underlain by permafrost and had a mean annual temperature of –10°C and an average yearly precipitation of 30 cm. The pre-fire vegetation composition of the study area was 54% moist acidic tundra (MAT), 15% moist non-acidic tundra, and 30% shrubland. The study focused on the MAT classification because of its wide distribution and because it had a higher immediate survivability than the other fuel types and therefore was able to provided a benchmark of pre-fire soil organic matter depth and plant biomass. Eleven MAT sites outside the burn area and 20 MAT sites within the burn were sampled. Sites were tested in order to compare pre-fire soil organic layer depth and depth versus bulk density, C or N concentrations, and to determine the radiocarbon date of the post-fire soil surface to see whether the fire burned into old and likely irreplaceable soil C pools. The objective was to observe the soil C and N content approximated at pre and post-fire locations to determine the emissions of the particular fire event and to put the results in context with a broader understanding of tundra biome historical norms and characteristics of the climate.

Independent of the transfer of C from the tundra soils to the atmosphere is the threat that any significant disturbances by wildfire have the potential to change local thresholds and alter the ecosystems structure and function through the alteration of surface reflectance (albedo) and energy balance of landscapes that are underlain by permafrost. For example, lake sediment cores showed that there was no observable wildfire activity within the study area over the past 5,000 years. A wildfire event of the magnitude of the Anaktuvuk River fire, has the potential to destabilize the underlying permafrost allowing it to release additional C into the atmosphere during the subsequent decomposition process (as a result of exposure), and adding significant potential for contributing to positive feedback to high-latitude warming. An additional important consideration are the increased concentrations of C stored at increased depths in peat soils, for when drying does occur in this fuel type, the fire doesn't only burn in a greater radius but can do more vertical damage as well in the semi-combustible soils; an image of the burn scar conveys this phenomenon very well. In this study in particular, though there were areas that had a soil depth range of 12.3–43.3 cm, the maximum burn scar areas were no greater than 15 cm in depth.

Mack *et al.* conclude that even a single surficially burning wildfire in the Arctic tundra biome can offset or even reverse biome-scale C uptake. Furthermore, C released into the atmosphere from fire occurs at a rate of 30–50 times greater than C release through natural decomposition mechanism such as, for example, stimulated soil organic matter decomposition from a 5°C increase in mean annual temperature. One possible implication raised by the authors is that changing local thresholds may lead to succession patterns that replace the current biome organic soil and vegetation composition with more shrubs. Such a shift would have the potential to ..."trigger additional positive feedbacks to climate warming because shrub-dominated ecosystems have higher productivity and plant biomass offset by lower soil C stocks." Although scientific knowledge and experience with the effects of fire in the Arctic tundra biome are very limited, an increase in this phenomenon has led studies such as this one to conclude that the possible near-future effects of fire in the Arctic can have catastrophic implications for atmospheric carbon levels as well as terrestrial carbon capturing and storing. As seen in the last 20 years, this dangerous positive feedback system of climate change is accentuated—from the high latitude warming resulting in melting snowpack and permafrost, retreating sea ice, to the drying-induced fire having varying consequences from albedo loss to instantaneous mass C releases from age old stocks.

High-severity Wildfire Effects on Carbon Stocks and Emissions in Fuels Treated and Untreated Forest

Forests contain the planet's largest terrestrial carbon stocks. Wildfires, by burning forests, release a significant amount of this stored carbon into the atmosphere extremely rapidly. This release interrupts a longer cycle where carbon is sequestered by growing trees and then is finally rereleased during the decomposition of the vegetation. Under forest management practices, forests have in many places been "treated" to lessen the effects of wildfires on tree mortality and to be better positioned to have higher survival during dangerous fires. In a study by North and Hurteau (2011), the short term effects of wildfire on carbon stocks were reviewed using field measurements, comparing treated and untreated forest areas in recent burn scars. The authors found that carbon emissions (during a fire) were more than double in treated areas. They further discovered that when the carbon release from the treating process was added to the emissions of wildfire in those same treated areas, the carbon emissions were significantly higher than untreated burned areas (93% tree mortality rate). This however is over a short time period, and that other studies suggest carbon emissions could be up to three times higher over an extended time of natural decomposition as opposed to the instantaneous carbon release induced by wildfire.

This study collected data from 12 fire sites in California (Region 5), mostly from recent burn scars in the northern Sierra Nevada. The area was chosen for its extensive use of fuels treatment practices by the U.S. Forest Service, which provided the necessary comparison basis for evaluating carbon emissions for treated and untreated fuels during wildfire events. The objective of this comparison was to assess differences in (1) carbon stocks, (2) carbon loss from treatments and wildfire, and (3) tree survival, mortality, and changes in live tree sizes and species composition. The selection areas were constrained to areas that fell under the practice of 'thin from below' prescription, through the use of machinery which creates 'machine piles' of slash (often discarded from logging operations) which are burned during favorable weather conditions. The study identified 20 treatment areas that had been treated within the past 5 years; the dominant fuel type was mixed-conifer. Areas where fuel treated projects had not been concluded by the onset of the wildfire (such as unburned machine piles), were excluded from the data.

Using the boundary of fuels treatment projects, 3–6 plots of 0.05 ha for ≥5 cm diameter at breast height (dbh) and 0.1 ha for trees ≥50cm dbh, were selected in both burned/treated and burned/untreated areas, usually measured within 200m from each other for consistency in fuel characteristics. Through a variety of methods, carbon content in treated and untreated stands was calculated as accurately as possible to best represent (estimate) carbon content before the fire to be paired with actual results after the fire. The study assumed that carbon concentration was 50% in woody material and 37% in duff and litter. It was determined that carbon emissions of the fire were 11% of the total stored carbon in treated areas while 25% in untreated areas. North and Hurteau found that on average, fuel treatment removed about 34% of total stored carbon. Additionally tree mortality as a result of the fire was on average 43% and 97% in treated and untreated stands, respectively. The authors determined that if the carbon emitted during the process of treating fuels (i.e. prescribed fire) were added to the wildfire emissions, the treated/burned fuels produced a higher mean net carbon loss (80.2Mg C ha 1) than the untreated/burned fuels (67.8Mg C ha 1). However, this is in the context of short term carbon releases, and the same fuels decomposing over an extended period of time will generally produce significantly higher overall carbon emissions. However, if logging operations were used in the treatment process, a part of that carbon store could be subtracted from the overall emissions for that area.

In treated areas wildfire intensity decreased significantly, and carbon loss and tree mortality was lower. Although the authors found that 75% of the forest carbon stocks still remained onsite after severe wildfires, up to 70% of ecosystem carbon became decomposing pools in untreated areas, with only 19% in treated areas. The overall effect was that regardless of fire severity, carbon sinks become carbon pools until the carbon sequestering of the re-growth process became greater than the carbon emissions from the decomposing stocks in the following decades.

In summary, North and Hurteau found that treated areas significantly reduced fire severity and consequent mortality and reduced the carbon emissions during the fire event specifically. However, when the emissions from the treatment process were added to those of the fire, carbon emissions were significantly higher than those produced by severe fire in untreated stands (logging excluded). This study was not intended to be extrapolated to entire fire perimeters due to the extremely variable burn conditions of these different fires; the pairs (treated/untreated) were matched to very small areas of each respective burn. Overall, fuels treatment was found to likely shorten the time until carbon was re-sequestered by stand growth, due to higher survivability. This study suggests that fuels treatment projects that reduce wildfire intensity, successfully reduce carbon emissions during wildfire events and over the long term, by reducing the amount of carbon emitting stocks in long term decomposing stages.

Interacting Disturbances: Wildfire Severity Affected by Stage of Forest Disease Invasion

The presence of disease in wildfire prone areas has generated the assumption that increased disease outbreaks result in increased fire severity. Studies suggest that this relationship is in fact more complex and empirical data show that fuel loading and disease stage are more indicative than merely the presence of disease alone. One challenge when evaluating the effects of disease on fire severity is that often no pre-fire data exist in infected areas, so mapping post-fire characteristics that are induced by pre-fire forest conditions becomes speculative. Metz *et al.* (2011) had the unique opportunity to observe the effects of Sudden Oak Death (SOD) on wildfire severity on the California Central Coast. They examined results from the 2008 Basin Complex [fire] that had a perimeter encompassing 98 of the 280 plots established in 2006 and 2007 to monitor the effects of SOD on the forest. They found that there was generally minimal difference in fire severity in SOD infested and non-infested plots, except that the more concentrated dead fuel loading on the ground in SOD areas did increase the effects of fire on soil characteristics. Furthermore, the minor effect of SOD on fire severity was more observable in areas that were in the early stages of SOD infections because of the high presence of dead leaves and small diameter branches in the canopy that had not yet fallen to the understory. These "light flashy fuels" can be very volatile when ignited and can increase fire severity.

Sudden Oak Death is an infectious pathogen that is increasingly affecting California coastal forests with high rates of tree mortality, resulting in increased dead fuel loading and altering overall fuel type characteristics; this has varied implications for forest management practices and wildland fire suppression tactics. An extensive network of forest monitoring plots in Big Sur California was able to provide more clarity to these causal uncertainties. The 280 forest monitoring plots were selected as 500-m^2 areas, wherein a variety of measurements and classifications were made such as vegetation basal areas (from diameter at breast height) to determine fuel loading, and estimated time since death and whether infection induced or not. The network of plots was established in 2006 and 2007. In 2008 the Basin Complex burned through 35% of the study area, and 61 of the plots were measured immediately after the fire in order to compile accurate data for the pre and post-fire stages. The purpose of the comparison was to answer the following questions: (1) Did pre-fire fuel loads vary among areas that differ in pathogen presence or impacts? (2) Was burn severity higher in areas that had previously experienced higher SOD mortality? (3)Does the stage of disease progression influence burn severity because of changes in fuels through time?

The forest plots were defined under two fuel types (redwood–tanoak and mixed evergreen) and were measured on pre and post-fire occasions to determine disease incidence, mortality, amount of coarse woody debris, and other physical and biological fuel characteristics. First, Mann-Whitney U tests were used on both fuel types to determine the composite burn index (CBI) in both pathogen infested and non infested plots. Secondly, further sequences of tests were performed to find, for example, if CBI increased in areas with higher basal areas of standing dead trees in infected plots; through this process the authors set about to determine some of the relationships of SOD induced fuel characteristics on wildfire severity. The 2006–2007 plot mortality data were used as a proxy for observing an increase of new host mortality, as well as to observe the progression of longer term SOD effects (downed logs) on fuel characteristics and subsequent fire severity.

The results indicated a variety of both anticipated general assumptions as well as slightly more unforeseen overall causal relationships to fire severity. First, Metz *et al.* found that standing basal area and downed log volume were significantly higher in pathogen infested plots; however, there was no significant difference in abundance of live or dead non-host species between infested and non-infested plot areas. Second, despite the increase in dead woody material of SOD-associated species, no significant increase in burn severity between infested and uninfested plots was observed. Third, the authors found that it was more constructive to evaluate the relationships between burn severity and fuel abundance when two categories were created; one for recent host mortality and one representing an older SOD presence. Recent host mortality is characterized by more fine dead fuels, while longer term infection is observed by more downed heavy fuels (logs). Overall burn severity had a positive linear correlation to higher fuel loadings, as opposed to the presence of the pathogen alone; presence of the pathogen was not indicative of the overall fuel loading. However, one positive linear correlation was found—that higher standing basal areas and downed log volumes in infested plots resulted in increased soil burn severity. Furthermore, it can be assumed that elevated soil burn severity has other implications such as post-fire soil and ash erosion effects on watersheds; however these were not explored in this study. Although SOD mortality does affect a portion of these forests, a significant importance for host fuel abundance in determining burn severity, was not found when infested and uninfested plots were compared.

A similar phenomena to SOD, is the bark beetle outbreaks in many other western forests that also results in areas of high tree mortality. For both these instances it has been widely assumed that there is a positive correlation between tree mortality and fire severity. For both these instances, we now have empirical results that suggest otherwise. This study is consistent with similar studies that suggest perhaps the most significant contributing trait of tree mortality to fire severity is the relationship of time from disease or pest outbreak to time of fire occurrence. In conclusion, Metz *et al.* cautioned that fire severity was not consistent throughout, due to the large variance in terrain, fuel availability, and weather characteristics at the time of the fire across all of their plots. Concerns that tree mortality significantly influences fire severity are still valid, as geographic areas not explicitly covered by this study can contain a wide variety of species, topographical feature, temperature ranges, and humidity gradients. Nevertheless, this study provides a rare data set for pre and post-fire forest characteristics in SOD infested areas. Further research in this area may be helpful in guiding management and policy decisions for addressing SOD and fire hazards in California forests.

Mapping Wildfire Evacuation Vulnerability in the Western US: the Limits of Infrastructure

In recent decades wildfire severity and occurrence has increased significantly due to a combination of climate change factors such as drought cycles, and population densities in fire prone areas. An increasing point of concern is the emergence of population centers within the wildland urban interface (WUI). This is the area where structures are integrated with or immediately surrounded by areas of moderate to high fire risk and are directly linked to fuel types and topographic features. When population centers in these areas have limited access routes, immediate egress in the event of a severe wildfire threat, becomes an additional hazard for these communities. Cova *et al.* (2011), focused on identifying some of these high risk communities in the eleven western states. The authors found that there was an inordinate quantity of high risk, densely populated communities with three or fewer evacuation routes in southern California as compared with the rest of the western United States. They imply that more attention should be paid during the planning and development of future communities in WUI areas, as well as taking certain fuels treatment measures to address safety in extant high risk WUI areas.

Climate conditions are increasingly blamed for an increase in wildfire severity and occurrence which has resulted in a high loss of structures and property damage over the past couple of decades. Furthermore, there are an estimated 12.5 million homes in what is considered to be the high risk, fire prone, wildland urban interface (WUI) in the western United States. Many communities are situated in the WUI but are not safely suited or adequately designed for a scenario in which an immediate, mass evacuation would be warranted due to a sudden severe threat of an approaching wildfire. This study projects a worst case scenario where most of a communities' population is at home (such as during night hours), and evaluates the number of egress routes (supply) against the number of households reliant upon them (demand). Cova *et al.* evaluated the eleven western states of AZ, CA, CO, ID, MT, NM, NV, OR, UT, WA, and WY, but divided CA into NoCal and SoCal for a total of 12 files. Important additional factors in evaluating risk include understanding fuel loading and fuel types, localized fire regimes, and identifying topographic features that enhance fire activity. The latter elements critically influence overall computed fire danger when coupled with the identified population centers.

The approach used for identifying these at-risk communities was a combination of initial heuristic assumptions, refined US 2000 census data, geographic information systems (GIS) data for identifying road networks and topography, and a previously established integer programming model. The programming model Critical Cluster Model (CCM) combines contiguous intersections—or "nodes", within a community (node set), with egress routes (exit links) in a pattern of arcs to extrapolate the maximum ratio of population-to-exits in a community. Constraints of the CCM were addressed through a region-growing algorithm. To acquire the initial data sets, a fire danger layer and a road network layer were applied; this resulted in the immediate removal of areas such as large cities or some desert areas where high fire danger/spread was not present, as well as all unpopulated areas. Through visual and computer generated location sorting, communities were identified that contained up to 100 contiguous intersections, had a minimum median fire hazard of 0.7 on a 0–1 scale, and had a minimum households-to-exit ration of 200 to one.

The computer generated results were grouped as communities with one, two, or three exits. These communities were then identified by state, number of nodes (intersections), and number of homes, fire hazard, and home-to-exit ratio. The highest home-to-exit ratios were then ranked within the three exit categories for identifying communities that exhibited the greatest concern for safety in an immediate egress situation. Cova *et al.* found that among all the western states,

171

Southern California consistently exhibited a disproportionately high prevalence of communities of very limited egress with high fire hazard and topographical restraints. For example, they compare a community in WA that had a home-to-exit ratio of 320.9 to 1 (3 exits, 962.7 homes), with a community in SoCal that had a home-to-exit ratio of 1,566.8 to 1 (3 exits, 4,700.3 homes).

This study provides the first rigorous analysis covering a broad geographic area, which identifies and compares low-egress communities in fire-prone areas in the West. The authors however, strongly caution against using these results beyond the initial enumeration and ranking of fire-prone, low-egress communities in the western United States. They identified a number of significant limitations of their methods and results, largely based on outdated US census data (2000) and the potential of serious miscalculation on the basis of inaccurate GIS street network data for individual communities. This study can however be valued in terms of demonstrating cases of unchecked development in the WUI with little regard to public safety and emergency planning. It can serve as encouragement to local governments to more seriously consider this relatively new threat to public safety and property, by an environmental concern that is noticeably being exacerbated through climate change.

Community-based Model for Bioenergy Production Coupled to Forest Land Management for Wildfire Control using Combined Heat and Power

With wildfires becoming more frequent and severe in North America and around the world, forest management plans have come under review in an effort to mitigate higher fire suppression costs as well as human and climate induced fire regime changes. When implementing forest management plans, small communities located deep within the wildland urban interface (WUI) are often left out of the equation for reasons largely to do with economies of scale.

Yablecki et al. (2011) developed a comprehensive approach to treating fuels to minimize the threat of wildfires in remote areas while using the biomass generated from the forest treatment process for electrical generation, making the communities more sustainable and self-sufficient. Additionally this community-based model afforded long term lowered utility costs and greenhouse gas (GHG) emission reductions. The authors conclude that their proposition combines wildfire mitigation through forest treatment, power generation through use of biomass, and all other associated benefits, in a model that is entirely managed by the community.

Using previously published work and available information, Yablecki et al. established and presented a general understanding of the wildfire threats and range of energy (acquisition) needs, and coupled them with common fuels treatment processes and costs per hectare under forest management plans in the USA and Canada. An estimated 20,000 communities have been identified in the US as vulnerable to wildfires, many of the most severely threatened and previously impacted, lying within the Wildland Urban Interface (WUI)—the area where communities integrate into forested land. In these areas there is less access (escape routes), more dangerous fuel loading in close proximity to homes, and in more remote areas, very limited fire suppression resources. This study postulates that reactive fire management plans are no longer effective, and that in addition to other factors, proactive fuel treatment is preferred to heighten public safety, reduce the high cost of fire suppression activities, and to limit the devastating effects of home and business loss. In more remote communities, the authors propose an all encompassing model to accomplish the aforementioned goals, through community involvement and innovation in sustainable design, while addressing other community needs such as energy generation. In order to partially offset the cost of the forest treatment processes which are to occur every 15 years (in any given area), the use of onsite bioenergy generation is proposed under three models; operating scenarios are illustrated for two of them.

The first aspect of this model was an evaluation of fuel treatment costs in threatened communities. Costs were determined to vary from a low of $130 per hectare for prescribed fire alone, to nearly $3,000 per hectare with a combination of prescribed fire and mechanical treatment. Although the cost of mechanical treatment was significantly higher, so are the secondary use options, and hence the potential for additional revenue. One commonly associated issue with mechanical treatment is the cost of transporting removed biomass to be processed offsite—something unfeasible for very remote areas. Because the proposed model makes use of biomass onsite, these costs are eliminated. Biomass that was required to meet energy needs under three energy generating system types, were based on estimates of total annual energy use within a given community. The fuels treatment plan was adjusted accordingly to produce a sufficient amount of biomass for the bioenergy systems; the preferred 15–20 year cycles (estimated time before fuel loading becomes hazardous again) was taken into account and the threat of wildfires was greatly reduced under the new management plan.

The three proposed energy generating systems all fall under the category of combined heat and power (CHP) systems, and are best suited for small scale operations; they are therefore of the more appropriate technologies for these remote communities (most often removed from the power grid to begin with). They are the small-scale CHP steam Rankine system, the organic Rankine cycle (ORC), and the entropic cycle. The small-scale steam Rankine system produces high pressure steam for electricity generation through a direct-fired biomass conversion system that uses a boiler. This system however has the highest capital cost and requires specialized labor. The ORC system, of which there is a proven model commercially available in Europe, has a lower environmental impact and a higher operating efficiency with a 10% (electrical) energy conversion rate. However, it uses a variety of working fluids as alternatives to water, many of which are very volatile. The final approach evaluated, and found to be most suitable, was the entropic cycle. This system uses a process combination of the ORC system and small scale Rankine system to have an overall conversion efficiency of 68% with 12% representing the electrical conversion portion. The entropic cycle is the safest option, does not require specialized labor, and is a closed loop system so it does not require external cooling components and is therefore smaller in size.

Yablecki et al. chose a base case community of 100 residents expending an estimated 240kW (from three small diesel generators) for the modeling exercise; they used data from small communities in British Columbia as reference. They ran two scenarios with the selected three models. The first scenario utilized the CHP systems at 75–100% operating capacity year-round, while using some energy derived from diesel generators to offset a small portion of unmet energy needs in peak times (i.e. winter). The second scenario utilized only biomass; therefore the biomass required as well as the radius of fuel treatment needed, was greater. Between all three CHP energy systems, the entropic system proved to have the lowest capital investment, the highest return, and the lowest biomass input requirements. It therefore had the lowest need for labor intensive treatment processes and the associated costs as well.

To evaluate the GHG emission reductions as a consequence of this community based CHP bioenergy production and forest management model, the authors replaced gasoline fueled vehicles with electrical plug-in hybrid vehicles. This new fleet of vehicles could derive all their power from the CHP system(s) while only minimally expanding the community bioenergy production model, simultaneously reducing the communities GHG emissions and their dependency on imported fuels. Finally, Yablecki et al. formulated a loose revenue model largely based on overall long term savings while highlighting the revenue streams under the two scenarios. The payback

175

periods under the Entropic and ORC systems were 18 and 24 years, respectively. Considered for example, were the fuels treatment costs per hectare (an average of $1389), and a fuel consumption of 4.8 L per 100km for the hybrid vehicles (PHEV60).

Though the authors cautioned against the variability possible when applying this model to different areas on different scales, they contend that it is a valuable comprehensive community-based solution that goes beyond just mitigating the often devastating effects of wildfires within the WUI in the US and Canada. Yablecki et al. suggest that this model revitalizes communities and addresses a host of issues from public safety, preventative forest fire mitigation practices in remote areas, and maintaining forest health, while reducing GHG emissions and dependence on imported fuels. Overall, this model, suited for small communities, is a sustainability and bioenergy model that uses mechanical forest treatment as its primary support and supply mechanism to provide a wide range of community benefits.

Conclusions

Increased drought episodes have become major drivers of increased fire activity as well as longer fire seasons. We saw that wildfire activity in Greece has visually been impacted by these annual and summer drought patterns. Furthermore, the current climate trajectory suggests that further similar trends will, affect the entire Mediterranean region. As China faces similar prospects, scientists hope that their studies can aide in shaping future fire management strategy and practice through knowledge of these future climate scenarios. They hope to accomplish that through improving activities such as prescribed burning and initial attack-phase fire suppression responses. The study that paid special attention to Alaska's severe 2004 fire season is a response to aims of recognizing conditions for severe fire events in order to aide in predicting efforts needed by fire suppression forces in near-future situations. In other areas of the world that have less sophisticated or regimented fire management policies and response mechanisms, conducting these studies provide a context for developing fire prevention practices and policies while suggesting continued work in the subject area in order to translate study results into functioning fire prevention and suppression models for their country (such as Portugal). A major issue in the western United States is the unchecked development in the WUI with little regard to public safety and emergency planning. The study by Cova *et al.* can serve as a strong case and encouragement to local governments to more seriously consider this relatively new threat to public safety and property, by an environmental concern that is noticeably being exacerbated through climate change. Ultimately though, governments whether local or national will need to take multifaceted approaches towards addressing these issues if they are going to be successful in guaranteeing public safely, economic stability and environmental protection. Although the small community model for bioenergy generation and forest management practices to provide a wide range of community benefits is not suited for all circumstances, it is proposed in the right spirit of ingenious problem solving and solution building—approaches policymakers should consider seriously.

References Cited

Cova, Thomas J., Theobald, David M., Norman III, John B., Siebeneck, Laura K., 2011. Mapping Wildfire Evacuation Vulnerability in the Western US: the Limits of Infrastructure. GeoJournal, Springer Science+Business Media B.V. 2011.

Dimitrakopoulos, Alexandros P., Vlahou, M., Anagnostopoulou, Ch. G., Mitsopoulos, I. D., 2011. Impact of drought on wildland fires in Greece: implications of climatic change? Springer Science+Business Media B.V. 2011. Climate Change.

IPCC, 2007: Summary for Policymakers. In: Climate Change 2007: The Physical Science Basis. Contribution of Working Group I to the Fourth Assessment Report of the Intergovernmental Panel on Climate Change [Solomon, S., D. Qin, M. Manning,Z. Chen, M. Marquis, K.B. Averyt, M.Tignor and H.L. Miller (eds.)]. Cambridge University Press, Cambridge, United Kingdom and New York, NY, USA.

Justino, Flavio, S. de Mélo, A., Setzer, A., Sismanoglu, R., Sediyama, G. C., Ribeiro, G. A., Machado, J. P., Sterl A. , 2010. Greenhouse gas induced changes in the fire risk in Brazil in ECHAM5/MPI-OM coupled climate model. Climatic Change (2011) 106, 285–302.

Mack, Michelle C., Bret-Harte, M. Syndonia, Hollingsworth, Teresa N., Jandt, Randi R., Schuur, Edward A. G., Shaver, Gaius R., Verbyla, David L., 2011. Carbon Loss from an Unprecedented Arctic Tundra Wildfire. *Nature* 475, 489–492.

Marques, S., Borges, J. G. J., Garcia-Gonzalo, Moreira, F., Carreiras, J. M. B., Oliveira, M. M., Cantarinha, A., Botequim, B., Pereira, J. M. C., 2011. Characterization of wildfires in Portugal. European Journal of Forest Research 130, 775–784.

Metz, Margaret R., Frangioso, Kerri M., Meentemeyer, Ross K., Rizzo, David M., 2011. Interacting disturbances: wildfire severity affected by stage of forest disease invasion. Ecological Applications 21, 313–320.

North, Malcolm P., Hurteau, Matthew D., 2011. High-severity wildfire effects on carbon stocks and emissions in fuels treated and untreated forest. Forest Ecology and Management 261, 1115–1120.

O'Donnell, Alison J., Boer, Matthias M., McCaw, W. Lachlan, and Grierson, Pauline F., 2011. Vegetation and landscape connectivity control wildfire intervals in unmanaged semi-arid shrublands and woodlandsin Australia. Journal of Biogeography 38, 112-124.

Wathen, Stephen F., 2011. 1,800 Years of abrupt climate change, severe fire, and accelerated erosion, Sierra Nevada, California, USA. Climatic Change 108, 333–356

Wendler, G., Conner, J., Moore, B., Shulski, M., Stuefer, M., 2010. Climatology of Alaskan wildfires with special emphasis on the extreme year of 2004. Theoretical and *Applied* Climatology (2011), 104:459–472

Xiao-rui, T., Li-fu, S., Feng-jun, Z., Ming-yu, W., McRae, Douglas J., 2011. Future impacts of climate change on forest fire danger in northeastern Chin. Journal of Forestry Research 22, 437–446.

Yablecki, Jessica, Bibeau, Eric L., Smith, Doug W., 2011. Community-based model for bioenergy production coupled to forest land management for wildfire control using combined heat and power. Biomass and Bioenergy 35, 2561–2569.

6. Human Migration and Climate Change

Adriane Holter

The topic of human migration and climate change in the environmental sciences is a relatively new, and therefore limited, field. Faced with the growing evidence of climate change, scientists have begun to direct concerted effort at understanding the ways in which environmental shifts impact human populations; however, the relationship between human movement and the state of the environment is one that has existed since the earliest days of the planet. Yet, this early relationship is not the one that still exists in the present. Rather, the degradation of the earth based on human action and policies has eroded previous means of environmental stability that humans depend on to sustain a safe and secure lifestyle.

To reflect the nuances of the present, this chapter begins with a look at scientific research into the history of human migration and climate change and then moves into current issues of ecology, equity, and policy. Due to the sparse nature of purely scientific information on the subject, supplemental reviews from other disciplines (e.g. economic, governmental) are also included. When considered in conjunction with each other, this group of articles presents the debate about the origins, consequences, and responsibilities of human migration and climate change from a variety of angles, while also highlighting several of the areas where gaps of knowledge and the need for future research exist.

Abrupt Holocene Climate Change as an Important Factor for Human Migration in West Greenland

Temperature fluctuations in West Greenland are known to have impacted human movement and migration during the Holocene period. However, due to the myriad of social, political, and economic reasons that humans move from land it is difficult to pinpoint how much temperature impacted the change in behavior. D'Andrea, Huang, Fritz, and Anderson et al. (2011) examined the relationship between temperature and migration of four groups that inhabited West Greenland during the Holocene period through the comparative study of sediment samples from two lakes. This method allowed researchers to compare the past state of temperature variability in West Greenland with historical records of human populations in the region. The study found that fluctuations in temperature did have a positive correlation with population shifts out of West Greenland. Importantly, this research helps provide examples of how climate change has shaped geological epochs of human history.

During the Holocene period, four groups of people lived in the West Greenland area: the Saqqaq (4,500 y B.P.), the Dorset (2,800–2,200 y B.P.), the Norse (650 y B.P.), and the Thule who still remain in the area to present. Throughout the Holocene period, the civilization of these four groups was substantially impacted by temperature change. For instance, access to resources and tools for acquiring such resources was greatly influenced by environmental conditions. Thus, an abrupt change in temperature had the potential to alter the lives of a population to a large enough degree that they left an area. In West Greenland, it is highly likely that Holocene temperature variability was a dominant force in population shifts.

During the time that the Saqqaq inhabited West Greenland, the region experienced an interval of warmth that then shifted into a transient period of warmth and cooling between the years 4,100 and 3,400 B.P. The authors hypothesize that an abrupt cooling of the region that occurred in 3,400 B.P. began to push the Saqqaq out of the Sisimiut region; however, it was not until further decrease in temperature in 2,800 B.P. that the group left the area completely. Thus, the magnitude of the temperature shift is an essential element of how humans experience climate change; rate of change alone does not determine human impact.

Unlike the Saqqaq, archaeological evidence from the Dorset population suggests that the group was better adapted to handle fluctuations in temperature. For instance, remnants of tools for sea-ice hunting suggest that the Dorset were well suited to cold weather conditions. It is more difficult to determine why the Dorset abandoned the region in 2,200 B.P instead of other periods of significant temperature change that occurred during the time they inhabited West Greenland. The unclear reasons for the migration of the Dorset remind us that theories of climate change produce only a partial explanation of human movement. Nevertheless, temperature shifts can partially explain why certain groups move into an area to begin with. The warming of West Greenland experienced from ca. 1,000 to 850 B.P. (roughly middle of the 14th century) is one probable reason that the Norse migrated to the region. Once again, lifestyle factors impacted how a population was impacted by climate change. A sedentary farming population, the Norse were less able to respond to temperature shifts and were therefore greatly impacted by the period of increased cooling from 850 until 630 B.P. when they abandoned West Greenland leaving the area free for the Thule to settle to the present day.

In order to establish these relationships between temperature and population in West Greenland, the researchers studied sediment cores from two lakes (Braya Sø and Lake E) that were 10 kilometers apart. By examining the alkonene levels in the sediment cores, the authors were able to reconstruct sea-level temperatures during thousands of years. This research was strengthened by the fact that previous studies have shown air temperature has a strong impact on sea-level temperature in West Greenland. The study indicates that temperature might have varied as much as 5.5°C in the Kangerlussuaq region over the past 5,600 years. Interestingly, the authors found that the temperature patterns in West Greenland were anti-correlated with other areas in the North Atlantic such as southwest Ireland.

Migration and Global Environmental Change

Tacoli (2011) uses a livelihood approach to understanding migration patterns in Burkina Faso, Ghana, Ecuador, and Nepal. The livelihood approach shares modeling similarities with the New Economics of Labour Migration approach and, as such, includes natural resources as a fundamental source of analysis for movement and mobility. Due to the incomplete nature of scientific information on the evolving state of global environmental change, the author promotes the idea that an understanding of human movement for environmental reasons is too subject to error to provide accuracy. Thus, established patterns of contextual, qualitative reasons for human migration are the most accurate for future predictions and adaptive scenarios.

It is interesting to note the argument and source of the paper. Although the author notes that the views in the project do not express any standard governmental opinion, the thrust of the argument focuses on policy issues in a way that isolates environmental factors from such a label. As such, the effects of environmental change are made to sound uncontrollable and therefore free from regulation. For example, the study refers to the scientific community's inability to attain baseline data for migration flows as one reason why it is questionable to use environmental analysis to promote the sole rationale for induced human migration. The uncertainty of environmental change in political debates may be one cause for such a characterization of its role in human migration as presented by a governmental source.

The core of the author's argument rests on the premise that human migration must be understood in full context in order to develop a competent coping mechanism to address the associated issues. To achieve substantive analysis, the author uses a non-static livelihood approach, meaning that new data and evolving living situations are considered and implemented into the report. Real world scenarios are then taken from previous studies in the four selected regions with the Burkina Faso and Nepal cases also looking at non-migrants, while the Ghana and Ecuador cases primarily consider migrant populations.

The main point of analysis is derived from the livelihood issues that surround any environmental reasons for migration discovered by any of the cited empirical studies. Human capital, defined as education and skills, has a large impact on movement, especially in rural-urban movement. Sustainability is also of similar importance. At the point where living conditions become unsustainable in a region, those persons who are able to migrate are better off than those who are unable and must then remain in unfavorable living conditions. It is thus necessary that non-migrants existing in geographic zones where large amounts of migration have occurred be treated as a vulnerable population. Ultimately, the author states that migration and human movement is on an increasing upswing from current rates with environmental change as a driving cause.

The author concludes by offering the recommendation that policy makers become aware of and attempt to implement programs that address the increasingly prevalent role of human movement in societies, remaining aware that economic considerations also greatly impact who moves and to where. On the national level, some countries, such as shown in the Nepal case study, have used the situation of human migration to create a national strategy of economic development. Ways to achieve the link between human movement, policy, and economic sustainability include education, access to markets, land holdings, and access to resources and labor. In order to avoid the impact of extreme migration patterns due to environmental disasters, policies adopted to appropriately address such a situation should also be developed.

Migration and Global Climate Change: Future Challenges and Opportunities

The final report on migration and global environmental change by the Government Office of Science London is based on the premise that human migration is driven by many factors and has equally many consequences, making it difficult to find a common policy recommendation for the issue. The five main drivers identified by the report illustrate the range of disciplinary fields involved in the subject of human migration: economic, social, political, demographic, and environmental; however, the authors of the report do distinguish between the conditional levels of support each category has in varied scenarios. On average, economic concerns have the greatest relative impact on human migration. Although often perceived as the most dominant, social factors usually come second to economic reasons for migration. In regard to environmental impact, deserts and dry lands are noted as exceptional regions where migration is a substantial concern for the sustainability of the livelihood and quality of life of human populations.

A desert dryland is defined as having limited soil moisture with low rainfall and high evaporation rates. These areas, totaling 40% of the earth's surface, are home to 2 billion people. Drylands are also subject to land degradation due to harsh environmental conditions and human activities such as agriculture. As a result of land degradation, the already limited natural resources in these arid regions diminish to levels where humans often are unable to sustain a comfortable existence and thus decide to migrate. These regions are also highly susceptible to sustained periods of drought, further imperiling human livelihoods. The researchers anticipate, through the study of temperature change and rainfall in Southern Africa, West Africa, North Africa, and Mexico, that since 1970 these regions have experienced a strong, steady increase in the number of people that have relocated. In comparison to the numbers leaving, a comparatively miniscule number of people are immigrating into or returning to these regions.

Overall, the researchers of the study seem to frame migration as a traditional social tool that has been adapted as a solution for the dilemmas posed to humans in rapidly deteriorating environments. Furthermore, many of the traditional drivers for human movement (e.g. economic and social) are the cause of pressures resulting from environmental conditions. Therefore, it is fair to state that ecological reasons account for a large majority of the drivers that cause human migration; however, the type of migration that may occur in any given scenario is subject to several factors. This study identifies two main types of migration: rural-to-rural migration aimed at diversifying social and economic opportunities and longer-distance migration. The former often lowers the likelihood of the latter, which requires economic capital to undertake. Perception is also identified as a crucial element for movement. If a person perceives a situation to be more dire than it truly is, she will respond as if the situation were indeed that dire. Thus, real and perceived impacts of climate change have the potential to create a lived impact on human demographics. The way in which these different modes and reasons for migration unfold is largely determined by the unique political and social structures within which they occur.

Additionally, the paper highlights the dilemma of 'trapped' populations that experience extreme impacts from climate change and are unable to plan migration due to these circumstances. The researchers recommend that due to its vulnerability, this group of people should be given priority for relief from policy makers. If policy responses are not made to correct for the dilemmas of 'trapped' populations and all those impacted by climate change, the researchers suggest that marginalized groups will be highly susceptible to extreme environmental events, conflict is likely to occur, and management will result in political upheaval and displacement. Well-researched and multi-disciplinary educated policy formulas are the best way to combat these projections of the future of climate change on human populations.

Geographic Disparities and Moral Hazards in the Predicted Impacts of Climate Change on Human Populations

It is well known in the scientific community that climate change will impact humans in many ways, depending on their location. However, the myriad of complex decision patterns for human reaction to climate change and the variability of regional impact often limits scientific analysis to qualitative analysis of the consequences of climate change. In response to this trend of study, Samson et al. (2011) studied the relationship between global distributions of human population density and climate to predict future regional climate vulnerabilities. Niche models were used to create this global index of the projected impacts of climate change on human populations by assessing how environmental niches would likely change or move based on shifts in climate. Human population density data were obtained from the Gridded Population of the World and then adjusted to United Nations national population size records, while climate forecast was taken from the WorldClim database. From these data, researchers identified Central America, Central South America, the Arabian Peninsula, Southeast Asia, and much of Africa as the regions whose populations are most vulnerable to the effects of climate change. Notably, these regions are far away from the high-latitude areas where it is estimated that climate change will be the greatest. The research also employed geographically weighted regression models to conceptualize the spatial element of the relationship between climate and humans.

The ecological niche model used in this projection was contrasted with CO_2 emissions data to quantitatively discern the concept of a moral hazard in climate change. This moral hazard reflects the relationship of the cause for and the predicted consequences of climate change. Interestingly, researchers found that the human populations that created the largest amount of greenhouse gases on a per capita basis were the least likely to experience the most severe effects of climate change. Researchers also found that the factors that cause regional climate change are correlated with the projected impact of climate change on human populations. Thus, a moral hazard exists on the level that those populations that produce the most green-house gas transmit the harmful byproduct onto other populations.

The research supports the intuitive theory that areas of the globe that are already dry will increase in dryness and become increasingly vulnerable. One reason for this vulnerability is the difficulty of food production in agricultural and pastoral societies when dryness decreases the amount of arable land. Conversely, cold areas with low population densities will be able to support larger future populations with the impact of climate change. It is extremely likely that climate change will result in new dispersals of human populations throughout the globe; however, we must also ask if reduced population densities in a given location are due to the inability of humans to live there or because they elect to leave. Regardless, these conclusions support the need for climate policy that responds to the predicted needs of those populations that will be most greatly influenced by climate change.

Adriane Holter

When Nature Rebels: International Migration, Climate Change, and Inequality

By combining economic models with environmental knowledge, the authors of this study sought to create an analysis of international human migration that encompassed policy responses to the issue. A two-country overlapping generations model with endogenous climate change measured on a scale of steady state perspective was used to accomplish this end. The authors summarize their main findings as follows: change in climate creates an increase in migration, small levels of climate change result in substantial impacts on the number of migrants, northern immigration policies have the potential to impact long-run migration thus impacting regional inequality, and finally that green technology decreases emissions and long-run migration where the migrant impact to climate change is significant. A consideration of how values of inequality, wealth, environment, and migration numbers impact policy development is also widely discussed. Although the authors caution that there are limitations to their approach, they ultimately advocate that their model may provide states with guidelines for how to best distribute tax revenue in regard to the issue of human migration.

In an environmental review, the authors remind that while the developed world is responsible for the vast majority of CO_2 emissions, it is the developed world that will experience 80% of the lived damage of global climate change. These experiences include the loss of agricultural productivity and water quality, resulting in unsustainable living conditions that oftentimes lead to environmentally motivated migration. Reasons for movement out of an area also may include anticipation of deteriorating and therefore non-sustainable living conditions. The economic model used in the study incorporates concerns of livelihood by presenting a decision calculus that states when a person considers the benefit of migration to be greater than that of staying at home, then that person will mi-grate. The firms in the model are stated as operating on the basis of profit maximization in a perfectly competitive market where they have access to international capital mobility.

The authors present four propositions that result from their analysis, many of which have important policy implications. First, the optimization consideration of firms combined with the relative situation of people creates an integrated approach that indicates the economic independence of the firm. Second, endogenous climate change is a large contributor to international migration that effec-tively diminishes the per capita welfare of both northern and south-ern regions. Third, increased allocation of funds toward border controls reduces southern access to migration and increases north-ern control. This relationship has the ability to either exaggerate or lessen current north-south regional inequalities due to environmen-tal improvements and long-run migrant numbers. Finally and simi-lar to the third proposition, an increase in taxes allocated to green technology will potentially decrease migrant numbers, positively impact the environment, and alter the relationship between north-south inequality.

Based on these propositions, the authors posit that it is more advisable for Europe to increase the allotment of tax revenue toward immigration costs than North America. Conversely, North America should invest more tax revenue in green technology than Europe. This inverse economic relationship is due to the fact that production in North America creates substantially larger numbers of CO_2 emissions than its European counterpart and therefore may best benefit from new environmental policy. Additionally, North America currently employs harsh restrictions on border control pol-icy. Europe's comparatively "soft" immigration policy therefore makes new approached commendable.

Adriane Holter

Drought and Other Driving Forces behind Population Change in Six Rural Counties in the United States

Although population change in the United States has been widely researched, most studies have focused on social and economic reasons for population shifts. The research that does exist on environmental factors for the most part has looked at temperature and seasonal relationships. To provide more depth to known impact of environment on US population shifts, Maxwell et al. (2011) set the primary research goal of identifying the main reasons for population shifts in six counties in three geographic regions. Secondarily, the researchers were interested in finding the relationship between drought from the 1800s to the present and population change. Furthermore, the study sought to assess the spatial variability between the six locations in the study. The study found that traditional variables for population change—unemployment, education, technological advancement, etc.—had the largest impact on population change. Through correlation and regression analysis drought was determined to cause a small variance in population change with significance in three of the six counties. Spatially, without other measures of climatic variables, counties in the same region tended to experience similar results.

The three regions observed in the study were: the Southeast, Ohio Valley, and Great Plains. The counties within these regions shared similar urban structures and economic makeups. All counties were predominately rural and agricultural. Studied counties did not have a metropolitan center, a highway that passed through the region, corporate owned farms, or substantial irrigation. Per capita income, agricultural prices, and manufacturing prices were acquired from census data and adjusted for inflation in order to analyze economic elements of population change. Additionally, variables such as birth and death rates, educational attainment, and unemployment were standardized by country population in the same year for use in developing a full social picture of each county. Climatic variables were retained from the National Climatic Data Center from 1985 to 2000. Drought was quantified through the study of tree rings in the Palmer Drought Severity Index (PDSI), which included an 11-year moving average to account for the extreme yearly variations in temperature and moisture. A multiple regression model was used to analyze which factors were the biggest drivers for population change in each county.

In the Southeast, the primary drivers for population change in Sampson County, North Carolina were manufacturing value with other significant factors in agricultural and educational sectors. In Bedford County, South-Central Tennessee the primary drivers were college attainment and temperature, with secondary influencers of agricultural value, manufacturing value, and high school attainment. Drought had a significant impact on population change, while population was inversely related to temperature. Increased level of educational attainment indicated an increase in population. In this area, the intuitive tie between drought and agriculture is evident–lower amounts of moisture negatively affect crops.

In the Ohio Valley, Adams County in Northeast Indiana the most successful model for population change included high school attainment, PDSI, and the death rate. Converse to the findings in the Southeast and Ohio Valley, Pottawatomie County, Northeast Kansas in the Great Plains had a negatively correlated relationship between college attainment and population. Similar to Adams County, PDSI has a significant impact on population change in Pottawatomie. Also in the Great Plains, Tillman County, Southwest Oklahoma had the key population change drivers of high school attainment and death rates with birth rates, college attainment, and annual income also possessing a strong influence. Finally, population change in Douglas County in southeastern South Dakota was most strongly linked to high school attainment and birth rates. Like Tillman County, the levels of death rates, college attainment, and annual income were also important factors.

The fact that population changes in three of the six counties researched in this study were positively related to the availability of moisture signals the need for more research in the relationship between drought and population size. Currently in the United States, the Southeast and the Southwest have the highest rate of population growth in the country. Furthermore, many of the counties in these regions still rely heavily on agriculture. With the increase in climate change, it is likely that droughts will become more frequent and intense today than the measures found in this study. The relationship between drought and threats to agricultural sustainability make these field a crucial realm of research.

Soil Quality and Human Migration in Uganda and Kenya

The issues of soil quality impact on humans and environmental migration have been highly debated in the scientific community. However, studies previously conducted on these issues have lacked a large-scale program to monitor soil-degradation. Furthermore, no study has examined economic or social concerns about soil quality outside of agriculture. With the intention to correct these oversights, Gray et al (2011) sought to measure how soil quality impacts internal migration from grain-producing households in the East African Highland countries of Uganda and Kenya. The results of the study show that out-migration from these counties declined with soil quality. Soil quality in Kenya was particularly relevant for migration in small farm households. In Uganda, there was an increase in marginal migration with soil quality, which is consistent with the poverty trap of migration where rural population is large and access to agricultural resources is limited. The authors of the study see their work as a necessary consideration for development policy in Kenya and Uganda.

To implement their study, Gray et al. used a longitudinal survey dataset with information collected through the Research on Poverty, Environment, and Agricultural Technology (REPEAT) project. This dataset contained information on migration and soil properties for 1200 households. From this information, the researchers created a household-level measure of soil quality as well as the rate that single persons undertook either temporary or permanent migration. A model of possible random effects tested the effect that soil quality had on migration with a control for household variables.

In Kenya, soil quality had a negative effect on migration. The likelihood for temporary labor migration was 67% lower and permanent labor migration was 42% less likely to occur when soil quality was high. Researchers found that women or married individuals were the most likely to undertake both temporary and permanent non-labor migration. This result is significant because it highlights how responses to soil degradation have gendered manifestations in society. Multiple attachments to several households as a result of marriage helps explain the increase in migration for married individuals. Additionally, migrants were stratified by age with the largest amount of movement occurring between 25 and 29-years-old except for permanent labor migration, which peaked between 35 and 49-years-old.

Since Uganda had a smaller sample size than Kenya, the results from the study are not as dramatic. Nevertheless, research in the country found that soil quality had a marginally positive effect on migration, especially for permanent non-labor migration. There was no clear gender divide for migration, but like Kenya age was also an issue in Uganda with temporary and permanent labor migration peaking between 30 and 34-years-old. Temporary non-labor migration was not affected by age. Also like Kenya, the likelihood of migration increased for married individuals. Importantly, individuals in both countries were less likely to migrate if they had been educated. This information reveals the socio-economic advantage afforded to the educated in the realm of migration, signaling a class-based element of the issue. Additionally, non-labor migration increased with a large number of inhabitants in a household and when the household owned large parcels of land. These results reflect the interplay of resource holdings with the need for human movement to sustain household livelihoods at a desired level.

Economic or Environmental Migration? The Push Factors in Niger

This paper examines the question of whether humans migrate for purely economic or environmental reasons. Although it is known that both factors impact human behavior, the complex decision calculus of humans makes it complicated to ascertain dominant causes for migration. In Niger, the poorest country out of a list of 182 on the Human Development Index, several important environmental push factors impact life: droughts, soil degradation, the shrinking of Lake Chad, Niger River problems, deforestation, and sand intrusion. These push factors are caused by climate change, regional ecological features, and human activity in the area. The authors of the study concluded that economics was the mechanism through which environmental impacts were felt by migrants, prompting the recommendation of the term "environmentally induced economic migration" to refer to the situation in Niger.

The sustainability of the environment is a security threat to the estimated 14 million people who live in Niger, because they rely on stable ecological conditions to maintain their livelihoods. With an economy that relies on subsistence crops, livestock, and uranium deposits, Niger's general population is at risk for destabilization due to rapid climate change. Studying the relationship between the environment, land, and the economy helps develop a more complete picture of the factors that contribute to migration in Niger.

To study the ways in which economy and environment interact, the Niger researchers combined a study of declining conditions with questionnaires, interviews, and phone calls to experts and migrants in affected areas. For the questionnaires, researchers polled 60 migrant and 20 non-migrant persons in a 2008 field visit to the regions of Niamey and Tillabeeri. Respondents to the research questionnaires revealed that: 90% migrated in part to some environmental consideration, 70% expected future environmental problems to impact them, 50% would migrate for or are currently planning to leave their homes for environmental reasons, and 80% would return to their homes if environmental conditions allowed. Although many of the people the researchers studied did not initially indicate the environment as the main cause of their departure, further examination revealed that economic rationale for migration had a root in environmental issues. For instance, the dwindling water for farmers and herders near Lake Chad directly impacted their economic security and therefore supplied a possible reason for moving. Thus, the term "environmentally induced economic migration" becomes valuable for conceptualizing the real world impacts of climate change.

Environmentally induced economic migration is a more permanent, uncontrollable situation than the historic cultural practice of seasonal migration in Niger. Furthermore, environmentally induced economic migration induces changes in social dynamics e.g. the organization of food source cooperatives and the selling of labor. Males in some regions depart during the dry season, leaving women and children to undertake the majority of work related to environmental problems. To help counter the social, economic, and security burdens of the people, the researchers recommended several courses of action including: development policies that prevent further environmental degradation, investment in the development of eco-friendly jobs, education campaigns for children and adults, emphasis on indigenous means of coping with environmental security threats, humanitarian aid for people living in abandoned regions, intensification and broadening of the President's Programme, and increased attention to the re-integration programme started by IOM Niamey for migrants motivated by the environment.

Conclusions

The interplay of human mobility with changed environment is a phenomenon rooted deep in the establishment of the distribution of peoples in various regions. It is important to note the historical precedent of this issue to better place the relative severity of current migration trends. Long range evolution of an environment and its suitability for human inhabitants is a natural scientific occurrence; however, the rapid onset of deteriorating environmental conditions due to the actions of humans is not.

It is commendable that the included authors have made the attempt to research and report on a topic previously left largely untouched by the scientific community. This level of attention alone seems to indicate a growing consciousness in the academic community of the plight of vulnerable migrants. Nevertheless, this attention must not be confused with the total amount of intellectual capital that may be directed toward human migration and climate change. To do so would rob the global community of information that has the potential to greatly impact the continued development of relief and policy reform—areas desperately needed if the issue of human migration and climate change wish to ever advance toward a stance of greater equity.

References Cited

Afifi, T., 2011. Economic or Environmental Migration? The Push Factors in Niger. International Migration published ahead of print May 19, 2011,doi:10.1111/j.1468-2435.2010.00644.x

D'Andrea, William J., Huang, Yungsong, Fritz, Sherilyn C., Anderson, John N., 2011. Abrupt Holocene climate change as an important factor for human migration in West Greenland. Proceedings of the National Academy of Sciences of the United States of America, 108: 9765–9769.

Foresight: Migration and Global Environmental Change, 2011. Final Project Report. The Government Office for Science, London.

Gray, Clark L., 2011. Soil quality and human migration in Uganda and Kenya. Global Environmental Change 21, 421–430

Marchiori, L., Schumacher, I., 2011. When nature rebels: international migration, climate change, and inequality. Population Economics 24, 569–600.

Maxwell, Justin T., Soule, Peter T., 2011. Drought and Other Driving Forces behind Population Change in Six Rural Counties in the United States. Southeast Geographer 51, 133–148

Samson, J., Berteaux, D., McGill, B. J., Humphries, M. M., 2011. Geographic Disparities and moral hazards in the predicted impacts of climate change on human populations. Global Ecology and Biogeography published ahead of print February 17, 2011,doi: 10.1111/j.1466-8238.2010.00632.x

Tacoli, C., 2011. Migration and Global Environmental Change. International Institute for Environment and Development: UK Government's Foresight Project.

7. The Future of Water Resources Shaped by Human Use and Climate Change

Darien C. Martin

Climate changes throughout the world will affect glacier volumes, sea level, precipitation patterns, and droughts. All of these factors determine how much water will be available for humans to use, and no civilization can survive without sufficient water. It provides for agricultural food supply, domestic uses, and industries. Many studies have assessed past trends and projections of climate change effects in addition to past trends and projections of human use in order to determine the amount of water supply loss and water supply stress humans may potentially suffer in the future.

The issue of water resources for human civilizations is something I have been interested in since I learned to farm and learned about different modes of irrigation, and water storage modes that affect our watershed environments. I wanted to see what likely outcomes of human activity and climate change on water availability might be in various places around the world. Globally, human water use is predicted to increase water supply stress as much or more than climate change. Increased volumes of water extracted from ground and surface sources will be lost to evapotranspiration (which is higher in crop than natural vegetation), and increased runoff into the ocean from land clearing for urban expansion and agriculture is expected.

Climate change is likely to increase severity and length of drought, and intensity of rainfall events when they do occur and is also likely to decrease the volumes of water stored in snow and glaciers. making water resources much harder to use in harmony with extreme weather cycles of water surplus and water scarcities. Increasing size and numbers of water storage systems to support growing populations in many regions can help, but may be insufficient if droughts are severe; severe water stress already exists in North America, Central America, South America, the Central West Coast of Africa, southern regions of Europe, and Asia (Voroosmarty *et al.* 2000*)*.

Effects will vary widely from one local region to the next due to climate and water use differences. For instance most of Russia is not predicted to have increased water stress. In China, the Yellow River may actually receive more discharge, while the neighboring Chin Jiang will receive less. Overall, weather extremes will make water management more difficult due to increased weather extremes. Improving water management practices, such as reusing water supplies, is key.

Predicted Global Water Stress Effected by Increasing Populations and Climate Change

Global warming and increased human population growth will affect future stresses on water resources. Voroosmarty *et al.* (2000) did a study predicting the effect of human economic and population growth and the effect of global warming consequences on the amount of water demand and water supply for 2025. They found that human population and economic growth will likely cause more water stress in future than the effects of global warming. However, climate change will likely interact with increasing demand to create more water stress than would otherwise happen .

Voroosmarty *et al.* evaluated sustainable water supplies, defined as runoff from rivers, above ground or in shallow aquifers, in the time frame of 1985–2025. They considered how water supplies would be affected with climate change, and collected data to detemine how these effects would interact with the effects of population fluctuations and industrial development. Water stress in regions around the world was characterized as the ratio of water removed from water bodies for human uses to the total amount of water available . Domestic and industrial water stress were measured separately from agricultural water stress, and both factors are also shown cobined.

Today, one third of the human world lives with water stress, and about 7.9% live under severe water supply stress. Western North America, Central America, central, south South America, Central West coast of Africa, and Southern regions of Europe and Asia all have severe water stress.

The authors estimated that industrial and agricultural water needs will be affected by population and industry growth than by climate change. The population that will be stressed both by population and industry growth and by climate change, will not be substantially larger than the population impacted solely by population growth and industry growth alone.

Voroosmarty *et al.* also collected data on the Yellow and Chin Jiang Rivers to demonstrate that conditions vary greatly even between regions in close proximity. In a figure which shows water stress increasing as distance from the river increases, the Yellow River population is calculated to be less stressed with climate change impact than the Chang Jiang River population is.

Climate change will limit water supplies in semi-arid and arid regions greatly, but population growth in cities and tropical climates is predicted to increase water stress more due to increased water pollution and demand.

Controlled Water Supply and Demand Studies of England and Wales Conducted by Water Companies

In the future, climate change in England and Wales will likely cause wetter winters and dryer summers. Along with other factors, the amount of useable water available will likely decrease overall while the demand for it will likely increase. Charlton and Arnell (2010) assess the balance of supply and demand in England and Wales from 2009–2010 to 2034–2035. The estimated decrease of useable water from 2009– 2035 is 520 Megaliters (Ml) per day and 475 Ml/day due to climate change. Climate change is shown to likely have the largest impact on water loss, with reductions in allowable water withdrawals to prevent environmental problems coming in second. Of the supply-demand water stress predicted, 37% will be caused by climate change and 56% by demand increases. Climate change could have such a high impact that most companies have agreed that it must be safe-guarded against and future plans must be made to access more water in the case of negative climate affects.

Twenty-one water companies compiled plans for 2009–2035. Data were gathered from 80 zones and were compiled and analyzed to predict the amount of impact climate change would have on water supply, and to compare this magnitude to other calculated impacts. The change in demand was then calculated using 55 of the 80 zones, and compared to supply. Lastly, companies' plans and options for future were discussed.

Each company surveyed its own resource zone and calculated the supply demand balance in its zone with the same equation:

useable output = available output – climate change impact – sustainability reduction (to protect the environment) – other reduc-tions– other allowances – process use loss – untreated water export + untreated water import – treated water export + treated water import.

Companies used this formula to determine available head-room—the amount of excess supply which is left unused—which can recharge supplies. The three tasks assigned to guide companies with formulating their water plans were: 1. Calculate river flows and levels of river when it is replenished in different seasons; 2. Calculate future water data (by plugging groundwater data into a simulation which will predict future output); 3. Calculate future estimates of water demand; 4. Predict future headroom in wet, medium, and dry conditions. Climate change is predicted to cause hotter summers and wetter winters.

In projections for 2034–35, climate change impact alone caused an increase of more than 5% in fewer than 20% of company resources zones. The greatest impact increases were seen in the southeast of up to 15–20% in 4 zones, and 10–15% in two zones. Small zones were impacted by climate change more generally. Other factors affected supply; the second highest impact change came from reductions of sustainable water use practices, and other affects projected were marginal in comparison (such as water exports, process losses, and other allowances). This study also showed that the impact of climate change in changing water supply in 2034–2035 was uncertain, but that the amount of impact possible was substantial and should definitely be accounted for in companies' future plans.

Water supply was evaluated from present to 2035, with concern given to useable output, climate change effect, sustainability reduction, outage allowance, process losses, water export, and water import. The amount of useable water was measured for three scenarios: wet, medium and dry climates. 10% loss of useable water was seen nationally. Fewer than 20% of zones had a reduction of more than 5% water supply. 58% of the water loss projected to be in the southeast of England. The total water loss predicted is equivalent to a large reservoir, holding 21,320 Ml which provides water for 1.65 million people. This poses a danger to England and Wales if they do not plan accordingly.

In relation to this loss in water, demand is projected to increase 620 Ml/d over the 55 zones. Climate change is the dominant factor in water stress accounting for 407Ml/d in these zones. A reduction in the sustainable practices required in England is the second largest impact, causing a loss of 80Ml/d in these regions. It is shown that in the case of a wetter climate scenario, some regions will have an increase in supply in the future, which could reduce the demandsupply pressure, however, this would be irrelevant, because companies would not be able to take this water.

Possible actions for future water company plans include storage and increased connectivity. Dams would have the capacity to store excess water in the increasingly wetter wet seasons. Companies are starting to make their systems more coherent and connect their grids to flow more smoothly between zones, and correspond more directly to the networks of the water flows themselves. These connections may reduce water use losses.

Charlton and Arnell estimated that Britain would have a loss of 520MI/d of water in the next 25 years. This is 3% of overall useable water supply. The great majority of this reduction prediction will be caused by climate change.

In total, future water supply is projected to decrease 1117Ml/d by 2034–2035 from climate change, and water companies must adapt. Companies plan to focus on water supply increase. Building more reservoirs, and connecting water systems across companies to make a more coherent grid that coincide with whole river and aquifer systems are options. Charlton and Arnell believe this would build more water resource resilience for England and Wales in dryer summers and other unforeseen circumstances.

Possible Solution to Increasing Water Stress in the Middle East

Many parts of the world have started using treated sewage water for reuse such as irrigation or even drinking water. There is much potential to implement aquifer storage recovery (ASR) systems that reuse treated effluent sewage (TSE). To recycle TSE in the Middle East, further knowledge and testing of system sites for water recycling, more secure safe, large storage places, site specific wells, and thorough monitoring of system sites is needed. The hydrogeologic data collected at this point is not extensive enough to determine how water will behave in many sites. Water can be used in the dry season from these storage sites, and many harmful compounds will start to break down over time. Maliva *et al.* (2011) show in this paper that TSE can be broken down to pure potable water.

In order to be cost-effective and help the Middle East meet its supply and demand with water, storage areas should provide long term holding capacity. Above ground systems don't meet this requirement. Storage tanks, which could hold enough water for longterm storage, would be too expensive, and surface reservoirs have large evaporative loss and demand lots of land. Underground storage in aquifers is best suited for the job. Managed aquifer recharge (MAR) is ideal; using wells or added surface water to fill aquifers keeps them at a high enough water pressure to prevent salt-water intrusion. In these systems, water can be is added and drawn from the same well, or added through infiltration basins.

Maliva *et al.* present two approaches to storage and recharge of water in the Middle East. Water can be either physically or chemically bounded. Physically bound storage is enclosed by essentially impermeable concrete or rock on bottom and sides, and adding water and increasing pressure maintain MAR. Chemically bounded ASR systems include a freshwater body injected into brackish water. Brackish water is flushed away and then only freshwater surrounds the well. A zone of mixed water forms between the two water qualities, but separation can be kept with the right levels of pressure.

Pathogenic microorganisms and chemical contaminants are found in TSE before treatment. Pathogenic microorganisms coming from animals' intestines are a top concern and can infect a person who is exposed only once. The decay or removal of these microorganisms in Middle East groundwater may take several days to weeks in these warm waters. Chemical contaminants are also found in aquifer water from industrial activity, wastewater, and treatment chemicals. Treatment chemicals react with compounds in the water to form disinfection byproducts (DBPs). Emerging chemical compound threats to health, which are not yet controlled, are called CECs. Technologies to identify CECs have recently started to improve, and are now being measured in groundwater, surface water and TSE. CECs are a threat to health throughout the world wherever humans go. A certain degree of treatment and tests is required before TSE is injected into ASR systems. Components of the wells and aquifers should be designed to be readily accessible so that the ASR system can continue to be tested at every step of its processes. Possible threats to water purity and recovery efficiency (the percent of freshwater able to be retrieved) include surrounding rocks of multiple porosity levels with irregularities such as fissures which can make water movement unpredictable.

TSE converted to potable water is believed to be pure, but is usually avoided for the time being. Possibilities for reuse include direct potable drinking water and indirect potable reuse such as irrigation. With TSE reused as drinking water, TSE would be properly treated and then integrated into the potable water systems. Many times adding it to freshwater then breaks down harmful compounds faster. But for now, keeping systems with TSE in them physically separated from pure water systems is the accepted practice. In Saudi Arabia, the Council of Leading Islamic Scholars agrees that TSE could be fully purified again to drink, and TSE potable water will likely go up in acceptance and even demand in the near future, especially in areas that have a dramatically dry season.

Some places are being considered for aquifer storage resource systems that incorporate TSE. In the United Arab Emirates, where conditions for underground storage are not ideal with high salinity and multiple amounts of rock porosities, ASR systems have been constructed in shallow, unconfined aquifers. The city of Abu Dhabi in the United Arab Emirates is testing a site for TSE incorporation, as is Riyadh, Saudi Arabia. There, the depleted Minjur aquifer is now filled with treated TSE water. Sites have also been tested in Kuwait.

Through testing of specific sites, it is likely that more ASR systems including treated TSE will emerge throughout the Middle

East with the increase of water demand. Especially arid regions with population growth will be in great need of more water and TSE may become an important source. Information on the hydrogeologic conditions for proper ASR systems incorporating TSE is limited, but growing. Procuring pure water supplies from TSE is very feasible areas around the Middle East are being tested for TSE purification and storage plans.

Algeria's New Plan; Growing Capacities of Desalinization Plants

Algeria has experienced harsh droughts over the past twenty years. The driest regions of the west have suffered the most. Algeria has experienced increasing water stress due to growing populations, industry, and water demands of each individual in dry conditions. Drouiche *et al.* (2011) evaluate the future of desalinization of both brackish and seawater in Algeria through 2015. After plans to create more reservoirs were deemed inadequate, the Algerian Government supported plans for large desalination projects. There are also plans to ship water inland from existing coastal dams on the coast inland as water supply from desalinization plants becomes available by the sea. Technology is improving, and making it a more realistic option for supplying large amounts of water around the world. Eleven large desalinating plants have been built in Algeria, and five more are underway.

A century ago, a long drought began and Algeria's Minister of Water Resources planned for dams to pump water from the foothills up to the High Plains. This would aim to relieve the problem of denser populations collecting along the coasts. However, the reservoir levels were sinking. After evaluation, it was decided that reservoirs wouldn't supply an adequate increase in water due to predictions of less rainfall, insufficient building of the dams, physical losses from dams, overuse of groundwater, uneven water distribution, and contaminated surface waters.

During the drought, 21 small desalinization sites were assembled which worked to help people through the drought. Future larger desalinization plans were then assessed and found to be cost effective, and provide more water, over the long run, than new dams would provide. Algeria has many coastal areas that would be able to utilize supplies from plants locally. Other benefits include a virtually endless supply, desalinization processes that don't pollute waterways, and technology that has advanced and become affordable. The Ministry of Water Resources plans to move water supply from coastal dams inland to the High Plains, and then use the desalinated seawater for the coastal populations.

Algeria started building desalinization plants in 2003. These were mostly built by oil companies, and used thermal techniques of multi-stage flash evaporation (MSF) and thermo-compression. The Algerian government planned a new desalinization program, using "Build, Own, Operate" contracts (except in Kahrama). This requires that the same people who design the plants build and manage them, so that plants built are less likely to experience operation glitches. The Algerian Water Authority and the Algerian Energy Company built 16 large plants, 11 of which are now complete. Each produces 100,000 to 500,000 m^3/day. Except for one in Arzew, and another being built in Hamma which both use Multi Stage Flash, all new plants use reverse osmosis. The largest seawater reverse osmosis plant is planned to be built in Maqtaa. When all plants are complete, they will produce 1,461 m^3/day of fresh water. Seventy percent of the produced freshwater is used for cities and homes and 27% is used for industry. From 2011 to 2015, water supply coming from the sea is expected to increase 2,433,000 m^3/day, and supply from brackish water by 248,000 m^3/day.

The world's desalination capacity is growing at a rate of 55% per year and can now produce 60 million m^3/day of desalinated water, and in 2015 is projected to grow to 100 million m^3/day. Now, 63.6% is made with a membrane process of reverse osmosis, and

34.8% using thermal processes. Algeria, Spain and Australia have the highest rate of desalination capacity growth in the world. Saudi Arabia, the U.S., and United Arab Emirates have built plants to make the highest capacities of desalinated water since 1945.

Algeria has a plan underway to become more resilient to its long droughts through an integrated plan of transporting water from the coastal dams to highlands, and implementing desalinization on the coasts; more water will be available to a growing population, and industry. In addition to this plan for 16 megaplants, The Algerian government has been subsidizing higher desalinated water costs to fix water prices.

Asia's Five Major Watersheds' Resources Threatened by Climate Change

Asia's has five major water basins all more than 2,000 m above sea level: the Indus, Brahmaputra, Ganges, Yangtze, and Yellow river basins. Together, these basins provide for rivers that provide water supply for more than 20% of the global population. Climate Change will bring changing trends in temperature and precipitation which will affect the amount of water available for people. The hydraulic conditions leading to a change in water availability will vary greatly from watershed to watershed, but overall, there will be a decrease in water equivalent to a supply for 4.5% of the total population served. The Indus and Brahmaputra basins will have the highest water discharge decreases, and due to increased rainfall, the Yellow is projected to have a slight increase in discharge.

To project water supplies for 2046–2065, Immerzeel *et al.* (2010) measured the amounts of discharge and water supply for each of these basins, and investigated the effects of meltwater volume from ice and snow on discharge downstream. They then predicted future changes in ice coverage, and used these data to project the discharge and resulting water supply from each water basin. Other components affecting water discharge were factored in, such as amount of precipitation, before predicting water resource availability.

In order to assess how ice and snow amounts effect discharge volumes, Immerzeel *et al.* used a Normalized Melt Index which is: snow and glacier discharge volume divided by downstream discharge. Upstream discharge was found using a snow melt runoff model, and downstream discharge was found by subtracting the amount of upstream glacier discharge that had evaporated. It was found that the Indus and Brahmaputra received the largest percentages of their discharge from glacier melt; especially the Brahmaputra with glacier melt of 151% of downstream discharge. To determine ice storage, a gravity model combined with precipitation trends was used. Both ice storage, was tested to predict past discharge amounts, and predictions were accurate in comparison to past numbers.

Next, Immerzeel *et al.* predicted ice volumes and discharge for each basin in 2046– 2065 using general circulation models, which include a number of climate change factors. These results were inconclusive, predicting a decrease in ice for the Ganges basin, and an increase for the Indus. Lastly, upstream water availability was assessed beside water demand in terms of crop yield and energy to project effects on future food supply.

The research found that discharge from all rivers would increase for a short period when glaciers shrank, but would then decrease in all basins except for the Yellow River, which had an overall increase of 9.5% water discharge upstream. Decrease in glacier area and water discharge was countered but not reversed (except in the case of the Yellow River), by increases in annual precipitation predicted. The decrease in discharge may cause the Bramaputra, Indus, and Ganges rivers to become seasonal. The Indus and Brahmaputra will be most affected by climate change due to the high percentage of their water supply coming from glacial melt.

This will create an overall stress on food supply. Population on the Yangtze is the largest, the Ganges is most densely populated, and the Indus, Ganges and Yangtze have the most agriculture to support. The Yellow River may provide for an increase in food availability from increased water supply, but the Indus and Brahmaputra are in danger due to their large irrigation networks fed largely by glacial melt.

Changes in Chinese Water Resources and their Effects on Agriculture Production

Piao *et al.* (2010) examined various climate change models extending to future projections of change, and predicted future changes in water supply available, and how these components will effect agricultural production. China produces agriculture for 22% of the world population on only 11% of its arable land. Its main crops are rice, wheat and maize. Northern and Northeast China are dryer, while Southern China is wetter. Trends will vary from region to region. Precipitation trend will experience opposite trends from Northeast to South. Glaciers melting and changes in precipitation will each affect available runoff differently. These changes will be paired with projected increasing demand for water with industrial and agricultural growth. Without taking into account CO_2 emissions, overall crop production is projected to decrease. This decrease, however, will be countered with new agricultural practices and technologies.

Since 1960, the climate of China has been increasing in temperature by about 0.04°C each winter and 0.01°C each summer. It is certain from models that a warming trend will occur, but uncertain whether it will increase in rate. Two models demonstrate an increase in summer warming which would increase evapotranspiration and decrease water supplies.

Water supply is affected by both precipitation and glaciermelt. There is no general precipitation change for the country, but regional trends were found. The north and northeast have been declining in precipitation in summer and autumn with 12% lost since 1960. The South has had increasing precipitation in summer and winter. Predictions for future precipitation trends are highly uncertain. More drought and flood are predicted for Northwest China and the Lower Yangtze River and less for the northeast and the northwest of the Yangtze. One scenario predicts longer drought periods in the Northeast and less in the Northwest, while another predicts a decrease of drought in the northeast. Piao *et al.* suggest that more thorough studies on soil moisture and droughts in the twentieth century would help to formulate a more accurate prediction.

A decrease in glacier recovery of ice every year is more certain than precipitation trends. This will cause more runoff in the spring and early summer, and less water in late summer for the first few decades, and result in an overall water loss of 10–67% by 2100. Runoff may peak around 2030–2050 from the reduction of ice, but will then decrease.

There are conflicting models that predict how yields will change over the next 40 years, extrapolated from data from the 1970s to 2000. Increase in temperature itself will benefit irrigated crops and hinder rain-fed crops. Rice will benefit from an expanded territory to be grown in. Temperature will also cause an increase in disease and pests' terrain as well. Overall climate change and water shortages alone are predicted to reduce crop production by 2050: 4–14% less rice, 2–20% less wheat, and 0–23% less maize. This may be countered by the fertilization of increased CO_2 concentrations, but CO_2 increases could be canceled by the harms of increased ozone exposure.

Overall crop reduction due to climate change and water stress from diminished supplies and increased demand is projected for agriculture in China. It is uncertain how precipitation trends will affect future water supplies, but glaciers are certainly predicted to shrink, eventually providing less water. Crop production overall will decrease, however large technological advancements are being made and could continue to prevent or delay pressures of climate change and water shortage.

Evaluations and Plans for Water Resources in Distrito Federal, Brazil

Lorz *et al.*'s (2011) study of the Distrito Federal (DF) region of Brazil has found that past change in water availability has been largely due to land use/cover change (LUCC) more than climate change, although climate also has an effect. DF covers 5,790km^2 and has a "Cerrado biome" with a savanna landscape, and dry seasons from the end of March through September. Agriculture has expanded since the 1970s. Agriculture requires high volumes of extra extractions surface and ground water, resulting in decrease of base flow discharge levels by 40–70% from the 1970s. While Agriculture also affects water quality, urban development has released the most pollution into watersheds. Water demands in DF are near their maximum capacities, and populations will likely grow along with urbanization and a resulting increase in lifestyles that demand more resources. DF, with 83% urban population is in need of an assessment for a future water plan that will limit water supply pollution, and with the recent increase in agriculture, a water system will need to obtain more water.

Past data were used along with new studies done by Lorz *et al.* for land cover/use change, climate change, and water cycling from groundwater, to surface, to resources. Lago Paranoá was evaluated as a case study of the effects of urban pollution. Twenty-one organic compounds were tracked in the lake's water at various sites.

Fifty-eight percent of the natural land was lost over 1954–1998, and additional land continues to be converted to agricultural and urban uses. Although no-tillage is practiced in DF, 90% of the agriculture is giant mechanized operations, which can contribute large amounts of fertilizer pollution into waterways, and use large amounts of water. From 2002-2007, agriculture land area increased 47%. Urban areas grew, mostly along roads, from 0.1% to 10.6% in 1954–2001.

Climate Change was studied in terms of changes in precipitation. From data in the past from 1961–1990 and other periods projected up to 2099, dry seasons are predicted to be longer, and wet seasons predicted to generate more rain at once, with an overall small decrease in annual precipitation.

Groundwater and stream water supplies will be affected. Groundwater effects, in the future, will depend on the type of storage infrastructure. More porous, shallow aquifer systems have a larger danger of becoming polluted than deeper ones. There has been a decrease in base flow discharge of streams, likely due to increased evapotranspiration of cultivated crops, increased water extraction for crops, increased water extraction for urban areas, and increased evaporation, from hard surfaces, in housing areas.

Water quality has not reached levels that are higher than regulated levels yet, but quality degradations are on the rise from sediments and organic compounds in waterways. Oxygen depletion from added organic compounds has also occurred with ammonium increase near urban areas and waste water treatment effluent.

Lago Paranoá's pollution levels have improved since its detrimental occurrence of eutrophication, in the 1970s. Now, in DF, a new step has been installed in wastewater treatment, to remove phosphorus, but the lake is still in danger from pollution. An increased urban population has ingested more pharmaceuticals that end up in the water. Organic compound pollution doesn't exceed standards now, but an increase in phosphorus concentrations is predicted. Pharmaceutical concentrations are lower than in European lakes, probably partially as a result of warm water temperatures and lots of UV radiation, which helps to degrade them.

It is suggested that there should be increased support for programs that continue to monitor pesticides, pharmaceuticals, sediment, and other urban pollutants in DF. In addition plans are encouraged to reclaim ruined sites, prevent erosion, and manage sediment. New technologies and green efforts will help to maintain water resources in a growing and urbanizing, Distrito Federal.

Compiling Data To Predict Future Water Supply and Demand in Russia

Russia's Shiklomanov *et al.* (2011) compiled data at the State Hydrological Institute from various sources on the past and future characteristics of renewable water supply. All federal districts were evaluated for existing data from 1930 to 2005, and then predictions were made into the year 2020. The distribution of resources is extremely uneven with around 30 times more water volume available in Eastern and Siberia federal district, than in Northwestern and Ural federal districts. Water use in Russia breaks down to 63% for industry, 22% municipal, and 15% for agriculture. The areas with the densest populations have a limited supply. In general, however, Russian water resources will increase, and efficiency in usage is predicted to continue to improve. An increase in water supply per capita is predicted for many regions, but due to increasing population and activity, and larger amounts of agricultural irrigation in southern regions, along with decrease in supply may decrease water availability.

Water resources in Russia have been increasing overall from 1936–2006; however, demand has as well. For past supply trends, data were collected from watersheds with limited human use. From 1983 to 2006, the groundwater supply increased from 17.9 km^3/yr to 400km3/year while the safe amount needed changed from 17.5 to 33.5km^3/year. Runoff has increased from 20–40% in the most regions. More of this runoff increase occurs during winter and fall. Runoff of freshwater into the Arctic Ocean has increased by 210km^3/year in the last 12 years. A direct correlation with this increase and the increase of air temperature has been observed.

Future water resources are expected to continue to increase (except in the South, Southwestern Siberia, and Chernozem Center federal districts.) To predict future changes in river discharge, data from the past 25 years were extrapolated with general circulation climate models, and climate change measured from already existing data. Overall, river runoff throughout the country is projected to increase 8–10%, however southern regions mentioned above will lose 5–15% of their runoff. In regions with increasing runoff, there will likely be more discharge especially during winter and summer, and to a lesser extent, during spring floods.

Overall use is likely to remain the same or decrease in northern regions and to remain the same or increase in southern regions. Municipal water consumption is projected to decrease from improved water use practices; 20% less will be used by 2020. Agricultural use will likely increase from 2005 to 2020, as more irrigation is added; however, irrigation expansion will not exceed levels from the 70's and 80's. Industrial water use, will likely decrease or remain the same due to increases in use of recycled water.

Supply is predicted to increase in regions with more than 95% of the water. The remaining 5% of regions are predicted to decrease have some of the densest populations. Improving water use practices will also help to create more water availability and help to minimize increases in industrial and domestic uses, however growing agriculture will still likely increase water shortages in agricultural regions.

Sub-humid to Arid Zones of the World Experiencing Increasing Groundwater Depletion and Withdrawals

Wada *et al.* (2010) bound that between 1960 and 2000, the amount of groundwater withdrawn and depleted from climate changes has increased in sub-humid to arid areas of the world. Measures of groundwater depletion and withdrawal found decreasing volumes of water percolating back underground, and decreasing groundwater. The results showed an increase of around 57 km^3 per year in groundwater depletion. This consists of 36 ±10% of the global groundwater withdrawn annually, 2 ± 0.6% of the annual recharge, 0.8 ± 0.1% annual global runoff, and 0.4 ± 0.06% of global evaporation. Though uncertain, this decrease in groundwater supplies is likely to present an added sea-level rise of 0.8 ± 0.1 mm per year. This study compiled by Wada *et al.* (2010) concerns only regions of sub-humid to arid climates.

When performing this study, uncertainties in the data set results were caused by a number of variables. Wada *et al.* did not know the specific location of wells or irrigation systems, and it was assumed that they were nearby where the water was used. It was also assumed that demand for water correlated with water use. Demand was used to calculate estimated groundwater use.

First, the volume of groundwater was measured using a model that determined the volume of groundwater recharge. Volumes of water were tracked among two soil layers, the groundwater layer below, evaporation, precipitation, and snowmelt. two soil levels above the groundwater layer, evaporation, precipitation and snowmelt. Regions were organized into grids of 0.5° latitude by 0.5°longitude when measured. In each grid, soil types, vegetation, surface water body shapes, and groundwater area depth were noted when measuring the cycling water volumes. Groundwater recharge was determined by the amount of water moving from the lower soil layer to groundwater storage.

Next, the volume of water withdrawn in each grid cell was determined. The International Groundwater Resources Assessment Centre's online database was used to determine the rate at which of groundwater was extracted in many countries. Water was extracted at higher rates in Northeast China, much of Europe, the US, Iran, India and Pakistan. The rate of extracted groundwater in 2000, in all semi-humid to arid climates, is 734 ± 82 km^3 per year.

Lastly, annual groundwater depletion from 1960 until 2000 was calculated by subtracting groundwater recharge from groundwater extraction. A significant global trend in increasing groundwater depletion was found. Most severely effected areas are in Iran, Yemen, Southeast Spain, the Central Valley of California, and Northeast

China.

Although uncertain due to offsets of reservoir storage, this increase in groundwater depletion is estimated to have caused 25±3% of the sea level rise per year. This was estimated using the volume of groundwater released from storage data and the amount of that will end up in the ocean through runoff and evaporation followed by precipitation; assuming that all other variables of climate stayed constant. Groundwater depletion trends will likely continue to increase in rates, and to cause sea levels to rise (Drouiche *et al.*).

Conclusions

Although impacts are unpredictable, it is apparent that overall increases in weather extremes along with increases in human development will call for revised and improved water management plans throughout the world. Adaption to wetter wet seasons and dryer dry seasons is key with engineering in tactics such as increased water reuse, and storage on the rise.

In general, areas that support agriculture are projected to suffer from the most water stress in terms of supply, whereas urban expansion has often added the most runoff pollution to water supplies. For example, China, a largely agricultural country, suffers the most from water shortages (Immerzeel *et al.*), while in Brazil, water pollution and eutrophication from the runoff of expanding cities with impermeable surfaces is a larger concern (Lorz *et al.*).

Areas that already suffer from drought and dry climates are more likely to have increased water shortages. According to Wada *et al.*'s study, groundwater tables have decreased in Arid to Sub-humid climate regions around the world due to their dry nature and increase in human use. Commonly, the most stressed areas are areas heavy with agricultural activity. China, for instance, supports 22 % of the population with just 11% of the world's arable land (Voroosmorty *et al.*). In Russia, water management practices are actually projected to decrease water use for industry, but still people will need to use more water to support a growing population agriculturally (Shiklomanov *et al.*).

It is essential that water management is re-engineered to support the most essential activities, such as agriculture, as water use and climate change are projected to reduce sources on land and instead, create sea level rise. Examples of moving forward to improved water management can be found, such as in the middle East where countries are beginning to accept the recycling and use of grey water, and Algeria is improving desalinization technology.

References Cited

Charlton, M., Arnell, N. 2010., 2010. Adapting to climate change impacts on water resources in England—an assessment of draft Water Resources Management Plans. Global Environmental Change, Human Policy and Dimensions. 21, 238–248.

Drouiche, N., Ghaffour, N., Naceur, M. Hacene, M., 2011. Reasons for the fast growing seawater desalination capacity in Algeria. Water Resources Management 25, 2743–2754. Immerzeel, W., Beek, L., Bierkens, M., 2010. Climate change will affect the asian water towers. Science AAAS 328, 1382–1385.

Lorz C, Abbt-Braun G, Bakker F, Borges P, Börnick H, Fortes L, Frimmel F, Gaffron A, Hebben N, Höfer R. 2011. Challenges of an integrated water resource management for the Distrito Federal, Western Central Brazil: climate, land-use and water resources. *Environmental Earth Sciences* 1-12.

Maliva, R., Missimer, T., Winslow, F., Herrmann, R., 2011. Aquifer storage and recovery of treated sewage effluent in the Middle East. Arabian Journal of Science and Engineering 36, 63–74.

Piao, Shilong et al. 2010. The impacts of climate change on water resourcesand agriculture in China. Nature 467, 43–51.

Shiklomanov, I., Babkin, V., Balonishnikov, Zh., 2011. Water resources, their use, and water availability in Russia: current estimates and forecasts. State Hydrological Institute. 38, 139–148.

Voroosmarty, C., Green, P., Salisbury, J., Lammers, R., 2000 Global water resources: vulnerability from climate change and population growth. Science 289, 284–288.

Wada Y, van Beek LPH, van Kempen CM, Reckman JWTM, Vasak S, Bierkens MFP. 2010. Global depletion of groundwater resources. Geophysical Research Letters 37:1–5.

About the Authors

The authors of this book are students at the Claremont Colleges. The book is a work product of Biology 165: Advanced Topics in Environmental Biology taught by Emil Morhardt in the W. M. Keck Science Department of Claremont McKenna, Pitzer, and Scripps Colleges. Each student picked a topic, did a full literature search, and selected nine papers, most written within the past year, that exemplified the state of the science.

Their task was to write journalistic summaries capturing the essence of the papers but eschewing technical terms to the extent possible—to become, in effect, science writers. The summaries were due weekly and were returned with editorial comments shortly thereafter. The chapters are compilations of the individual summaries with additional introductory and conclusionary material.

The editor is Roberts Professor of Environmental Biology at Claremont McKenna, Pitzer, and Scripps colleges, and Director of the Roberts Environmental Center at Claremont McKenna College. He remembers how difficult it is to learn to write and appreciates the professionalism shown by these students.

Index

www.ingramcontent.com/pod-product-compliance
Lightning Source LLC
Chambersburg PA
CBHW062218270326
41930CB00009B/1772